D0668596

Dutch
Phrase Book
&
Dictionary

Berlitz Publishing
New York   Munich   Singapore

Contacting the Editors
Every effort has been made to provide accurate information in this publication, but changes are inevitable. The publisher cannot be responsible for any resulting loss, inconvenience or injury. We would appreciate it if readers would call our attention to any errors or outdated information. We also welcome your suggestions; if you come across a relevant expression not in our phrase book, please contact us: Berlitz Publishing, 193 Morris Avenue, Springfield, NJ 07081, USA. Email: comments@berlitzbooks.com

Fourth Printing: July 2010
Printed in China by CTPS

Publishing Director: Sheryl Olinsky Borg
Senior Editor/Project Manager: Lorraine Sova
Dutch Editors: Agnes Marston, Romke Rijpkema
Composition: Datagrafix, Inc.
Cover Design: Claudia Petrilli
Interior Design: Derrick Lim, Juergen Bartz
Production Manager: Elizabeth Gaynor
Cover Photo: © San Rostro/age fotostock
Interior Photos: p. 12 © Studio Fourteen/Brand X Pictures/age fotostock; p. 17 © European Central Bank; p. 24 © Pixtal/age fotostock; p. 37 © Corbis/fotosearch.com; p. 47 © Ryan McVay/Photodisc/age fotostock; p. 53 © Quendi Language Services; p. 55 © Stockbyte Photography/2002-07 Veer Incorporated; p.69 © Quendi Language Services; p. 73 © Javier Larrea/Pixtal/age fotostock; p. 75 © Netfalls/2003-2007 Shutterstock, Inc.; p. 99 © Getty Images/Ryan McVay; p. 103 © Imageshop.com; p. 107 © image100/Corbis; p. 109, 111, 114, 120, 129 © 2007 Jupiterimages Corporation; p. 136 © Jupiterimages/Brand X/Corbis; p. 138 © Stockbyte/Fotosearch.com; p. 141 © Corbis/2006 JupiterImages Corporation; p.143 © David McKee/2003-2007 Shutterstock, Inc.; p. 144, 151, 161 © 2007 Jupiterimages Corporation; inside back cover: © H.W.A.C.

Contents

Survival —————————————————

Food

People

Fun

Special Needs

Resources

Dictionary

Pronunciation

This section is designed to make you familiar with the sounds of
Dutch by using our simplified phonetic transcription. You'll find the
pronunciation of the Dutch letters and sounds explained below,
together with their "imitated" equivalents. This system is used
throughout the phrase book: simply read the pronunciation as if it
were English, noting any special rules below.

Stress has been indicated in the phonetic transcription with
underlining.

Consonants

Letter	Approximate Pronunciation	Symbol	Example	Pronunciation
ch	ch as in loch	kh	**nacht**	nahkht
d	1. as in English	d	**dag**	dahkh
	2. t as in cat if at the end of a word	t	**bed**	beht
g	ch as in loch	kh	**groot**	khroat
j	y as in yes	y	**ja**	yaa
r	r as in ran, but rolled	r	**rijst**	riest
s	always hard as in pass	s	**stop**	stohp
sch	s followed by ch as in loch	skh	**schrijven**	skhrie·vuhn
v	f as in fan	f	**vader**	faa·duhr
w	v as in van	v	**water**	vaa·tuhr

Letters b, c, f, h, k, l, m, n, p, q, t, x, y, z are generally pronounced
as in English.

Vowels

Letter	Approximate Pronunciation	Symbol	Example	Pronunciation
a	a as in father	ah	**nacht**	nahkht
aa	aa as in aardvark	aa	**maar**	maar
e	1. e as in red	eh	**bed**	beht
	2. u as in up	uh	**meneer**	muh·<u>nayr</u>
ë	u as in up	uh	**drieën**	<u>dree·yuhn</u>
ee	ay as in hay	ay	**nee**	nay
i	1. i as in bit	ih	**kind**	kihnt
	2. ee as in seen	ee	**mini**	<u>mee</u>·nee
o	o as in not	oh	**pot**	poht
oo	oa as in boat	oa	**roos**	roas
u	1. u as in up	uh	**bus**	buhs
	2. ew as in new	ew	**nu**	new
uu	ew as in new	ew	**duur**	dewr

Vowel Combinations

Letter	Approximate Pronunciation	Symbol	Example	Pronunciation
ie	ee as in seen	ee	**zien**	zeen
ei*	ie as in tie	ie	**klein**	klien
ij**	1. ie as in tie	ie	**wij**	wie
	2. u as in up	uh	**lelijk**	<u>lay</u>·luhk
oe	oo as in too	oo	**hoeveel**	<u>hoo</u>·fayl

---

* Called **korte ei** (short i).
** Called **lange ij** (long i).

Letter	Approximate Pronunciation	Symbol	Example	Pronunciation
ou, au	ow in now	ow	**koud**	kowt
			auto	ow·toa
eu	u as in murky	u	**deur**	dur
ui	aw as in awe	aw	**huis**	haws

i Dutch has many vowel sounds, and some may be unfamiliar to your ear. The best approximation is provided above, but try to listen to Dutch speakers to begin to develop accuracy in pronunciation.

i Dutch counts over 20 million speakers worldwide and is the principal language of **Nederland** (the Netherlands), often incorrectly referred to as Holland (North-Holland and South-Holland are Dutch provinces). Linguistically, Dutch is closely related to English and German, and you'll find that the majority of the population has at least basic knowledge of English. This shouldn't stop you from practicing your Dutch; your efforts will be greatly appreciated.

The Flemish dialect is an official language in **België** (Belgium). Though Dutch and Flemish differ somewhat in vocabulary and pronunciation, each is easily understood by speakers of the other. Both Belgium and the Netherlands use a common literary language, Standard Dutch.

Dutch is an official language in some of its current and former territories, such as the Netherlands Antilles and Suriname. Dutch is also the parent language of Afrikaans, one of the South Africa's official language.

How to Use This Book

These are the most essential phrases in each section.

Sometimes you see two alternatives in italics, separated by a slash. Choose the one that's right for your situation.

Essential

I'm here on *vacation [holiday]/business*.	**Ik ben hier *met vakantie/voor zaken*.** ihk behn heer *meht faa·kahn·see/foar zaa·kuhn*
I'm going to…	**Ik ga naar…** ihk khaa naar…
I'm staying at the… Hotel.	**Ik logeer in Hotel…** ihk loa·zhayr ihn hoa·tehl…

You May See…

DOUANE	customs
BELASTINGVRIJE GOEDEREN	duty-free goods
AANGIFTE GOEDEREN	goods to declare

Ticketing

When's…to Amsterdam?	**Wanneer vertrekt…naar Amsterdam?** vah·nayr fuhr·trehkt …naar ahm·stuhr·dahm
– the (first) bus	**– de (eerste) bus** duh (ayr·stuh) buhs
– the (next) flight	**– de (volgende) vlucht** duh (fohl·khuhn·duh) fluhkht
– the (last) train	**– de (laatste) trein** duh (laat·stuh) trien

Words you may see are shown in *You May See* boxes.

Any of the words or phrases preceded by dashes can be plugged into the sentence above.

Dutch phrases appear in red.

Read the simplified pronunciation as if it were English. For more on pronunciation, see page 7.

Relationships

I'm in a relationship.	**ik heb een relatie.**	ihk hehp uhn ray·laat·see
I'm widowed.	**Ik ben *weduwnaar* ♂ */weduwe* ♀.**	ihk behn *vay·dew·naar* ♂ */vay·dew·uh* ♀
Do you have *children/ grandchildren*?	**Heeft u *kindere*** *kihn·duh·ruhn/klie*	
When's your birthday?	**Wanneer bent u**	yaa·rikh
How old are you?	**Hoe oud bent u?**	hoo owt behnt ew
I'm...	**Ik ben...**	ihk behn...

When different gender forms apply, the masculine form is followed by ♂; feminine by ♀.

▶ For numbers, see page 158.

The arrow indicates a cross reference where you'll find related phrases.

Information boxes contain relevant country, culture and language tips.

i When addressing people you don't know, use **u** (formal you) or **meneer** (sir) and **mevrouw** (ma'am or madam), particularly with strangers and older people. It is impolite to address someone with the familiar **jij** and **je** (**jullie**, in the plural) until asked.

You May Hear...

Ik spreek slechts weinig Engels. ihk sprayk slehkhts vie·nihkh ehng·uhls

I only speak a little English.

Ik spreek geen Engels. ihk sprayk khayn ehng·uhls

I don't speak English.

Expressions you may hear are shown in *You May Hear* boxes.

Color-coded side bars identify each section of the book.

▼ Survival

Arrival and Departure

Essential

I'm here on *vacation [holiday]/business*.	**Ik ben hier *met vakantie/voor zaken*.** ihk behn heer *meht faa-kahn-see/foar zaa-kuhn*
I'm going to…	**Ik ga naar…** ihk khaa naar…
I'm staying at the… Hotel.	**Ik logeer in Hotel…** ihk loa-zhayr ihn hoa-tehl…

You May Hear…

Uw *kaartje/paspoort*, alstublieft. ew *kaart-yuh/pahs-poart* ahls-tew-bleeft	Your *ticket/passport*, please.
Wat is het doel van uw verblijf? vaht ihs heht dool fahn ew fehr-blief	What's the purpose of your visit?
Waar logeert u? vaar loa-zhayrt ew	Where are you staying?
Hoe lang blijft u? hoo lahng blieft ew	How long are you staying?
Met wie bent u? meht vee behnt ew	Who are you with?

Passport Control and Customs

I'm just passing through.	**Ik ben op doorreis.** ihk behn ohp doar-ries
I'd like to declare…	**Ik wil graag…aangeven.** ihk vihl khraakh…aan-khay-fuhn
I have nothing to declare.	**Ik heb niets aan te geven.** ihk hehp neets aan tuh khay-fuhn

Heeft u iets aan te geven? hayft ew eets <u>aan</u> tuh <u>khay</u>·fuhn — Do you have anything to declare?

Hierover moet u accijns betalen. heer·<u>oa</u>·fuhr moot ew ahk·<u>siens</u> buh·<u>taa</u>·luhn — You must pay duty on this.

Kunt u deze tas even openmaken? kuhnt ew <u>day</u>·zuh tahs <u>ay</u>·fuhn <u>oa</u>·puhn <u>maa</u>·kuhn — Can you open this bag?

You May See...

DOUANE	customs
BELASTINGVRIJE GOEDEREN	duty-free goods
AANGIFTE GOEDEREN	goods to declare
NIETS AAN TE GEVEN	nothing to declare
PASPOORTCONTROLE	passport control
POLITIE	police

Money and Banking

Essential

Where's...?	**Waar is...?** vaar ihs...
– the ATM	– **de geldautomaat** duh <u>khehlt</u>·ow·toa·maat
– the bank	– **de bank** duh bahngk
– the currency exchange office	– **het geldwisselkantoor** heht <u>khehlt</u>·vihs·suhl·kahn·<u>toar</u>

What time does the bank *open/close*?	**Hoe laat gaat de bank *open/dicht*?** hoo laat khaat duh bahngk *oa*·puhn/*dihkht*
I'd like to change some *dollars/pounds* into euros.	**Ik wil graag wat *dollars/ponden* in euro's omwisselen.** ihk vihl khraakh vaht *dohl*·lahrs/*pohn*·duhn ihn u·roas ohm·vihs·suh·luhn
I want to cash some traveler's checks [cheques].	**Ik wil wat reischeques verzilveren.** ihk vihl vaht *ries*·shehks fuhr·*zihl*·fuhr·uhn

ATM, Bank and Currency Exchange —————

Can I exchange foreign currency here?	**Kan ik hier buitenlands geld wisselen?** kahn ihk heer *baw*·tuhn·lahnds khelt *vih*·suh·luhn
What's the exchange rate?	**Wat is de wisselkoers?** vaht ihs duh *vih*·suhl·koors
How much commission do you charge?	**Hoeveel commissie berekent u?** *hoo*·fayl kohm·*mihs*·see buh·*ray*·kuhnt ew
I've lost my traveler's checks [cheques].	**Ik heb mijn reischeques verloren.** ihk hehp mien *ries*·shehks fuhr·*loa*·ruhn
My card was lost.	**Ik ben mijn kaart kwijt.** ihk behn mien kaart kwiet
My credit card has been stolen.	**Mijn creditcard is gestolen.** mien *kreh*·diht·kahrt ihs khuh·*stoa*·luhn
My card doesn't work.	**Mijn kaart doet het niet.** mien kaart doot heht neet

▶ For numbers, see page 158.

You May See…

VOER UW PAS IN	insert card
STOP	cancel
CORR	clear
OK	enter
PIN	PIN
GELD OPNEMEN	withdraw funds
VAN BETAALREKENING	from checking [current account]
VAN SPAARREKENING	from savings
KWITANTIE	receipt

Cash can be obtained from **geldautomaten** (ATMs), which are located throughout the Netherlands. Some debit cards (with the Cirrus, EC or Maestro logo) and most major credit cards are accepted. Be sure you know your PIN and whether it is compatible with European machines, which usually expect a four-digit, numeric code. ATMs offer good exchanges rates, though there may be some hidden fees.

GWK (Grenswisselkantoren), a Dutch financial company, offers foreign exchange, international transfer and traveler's check services. Exchanging foreign currency in a bank is another option. Though business hours differ between banks, most are open Tuesday–Friday from 9 a.m. to 4 p.m. and Monday starting at 1 p.m.

You May See...

Dutch currency is the **euro**, divided into **cents**.

Bills: 5, 10, 20, 50, 100, 500 **euro**

Coins: 1, 2, 5, 10, 20, 50 **cents** and 1 and 2 **euro**

Essential

How do I get to town?	**Hoe kom ik in de stad?** hoo kohm ihk ihn duh staht
Where's…?	**Waar is…?** vaar ihs…
– the airport	**– het vliegveld** heht fleekh·fehlt
– the train [railway] station	**– het station** heht staa·shohn
– the bus station	**– het busstation** heht buhs·staa·shohn
– the subway [underground] station	**– het metrostation** heht may·troa·staa·shohn
How far is it?	**Hoe ver is het?** hoo fehr ihs heht
Where can I buy tickets?	**Waar kan ik kaartjes kopen?** vaar kahn ihk kaart·yuhs koa·puhn
A *one-way [single]/ round-trip [return]* ticket.	**Enkeltje/Retourtje.** ehng·kuhl·tyuh/ ruh·toor·tyuh
How much?	**Hoeveel kost het?** hoo·fayl kohst heht
Are there any discounts?	**Kan ik korting krijgen?** kahn ihk kohr·tihng krie·khuhn
Which *gate/line*?	**Welke *gate/lijn*?** vehl·kuh gayt/lien
Which platform?	**Welk spoor?** vehlk spoar
Where can I get a taxi?	**Waar kan ik een taxi krijgen?** vaar kahn ihk uhn tahk·see krie·khuhn
Could you take me to this address?	**Kunt u me naar dit adres brengen?** kuhnt ew muh naar diht ah·drehs brehng·uhn

| Where can I rent a car? | **Waar kan ik een auto huren?** vaar kahn ihk uhn ow·toa hew·ruhn |
| Can I have a map? | **Heeft u een kaart voor mij?** hayft ew uhn kaart foar mie |

Ticketing

When's…to Amsterdam?	**Wanneer vertrekt…naar Amsterdam?** vah·nayr fuhr·trehkt …naar ahm·stuhr·dahm
– the (first) bus	**– de (eerste) bus** duh (ayr·stuh) buhs
– the (next) flight	**– de (volgende) vlucht** duh (fohl·khuhn·duh) fluhkht
– the (last) train	**– de (laatste) trein** duh (laat·stuh) trien
One ticket/Two tickets, please.	***Eén kaartje/Twee kaartjes,* alstublieft.** ayn kaart·yuh/tway kaart·yuhs ahl·stew·bleeft
For *today/tomorrow.*	**Voor *vandaag/morgen.*** foar fahn·daakh/ mohr·khuhn

► For days, see page 161.
► For time, see page 160.

A *one-way [single]/ round-trip [return]* ticket.	**Enkeltje/Retourtje.** ehng·kuhl·tyuh/ ruh·toor·tyuh
A *first-class/economy-class* ticket.	**Kaartje *eerste klas/tweede klas.*** kaart·yuh ayr·stuh klahs/tway·duh klahs
How much?	**Hoeveel kost het?** hoo·fayl kohst heht
Is there a discount for…?	**Is er korting voor…?** is ehr kohr·tihng foar…
– children	**– kinderen** kihn·duh·ruhn
– students	**– studenten** stew·dehn·tuhn
– senior citizens	**– ouderen** ow·duh·ruhn

19

I have an e-ticket.	**Ik heb een e-ticket.** ihk hehp uhn <u>ee</u>·tih·kuht
Can I buy a ticket on the *bus/train*?	**Kan ik in de *bus/trein* een kaartje kopen?** kahn ihk ihn duh *buhs/trien* uhn <u>kaart</u>·yuh <u>koa</u>·puhn
I'd like to...my reservation.	**Ik wil graag mijn reservering...** ihk vihl khraakh mien ray·zehr·<u>vay</u>·rihng...
– cancel	**– annuleren** ah·new·<u>lay</u>·ruhn
– change	**– wijzigen** <u>vie</u>·zih·khuhn
– confirm	**– bevestigen** buh·<u>fehs</u>·tih·khuhn

Plane

Getting to the Airport

How much is a taxi to the airport?	**Hoeveel kost een taxi naar het vliegveld?** <u>hoo</u>·fayl kohst uhn <u>tahk</u>·see naar heht <u>fleekh</u>·fehlt
To...Airport, please.	**Naar...Airport, alstublieft.** naar...<u>air</u>·pohrt ahls·tew·<u>bleeft</u>
My airline is...	**Ik vlieg met...** ihk fleekh meht...
My flight leaves at...	**Mijn vlucht vertrekt om...** mien fluhkht fuhr·<u>trehkt</u> ohm...

▶ For time, see page 160.

I'm in a rush.	**Ik heb haast.** ihk hehp haast
Can you take an alternate route?	**Kunt u een andere route nemen?** kuhnt ew uhn <u>ahn</u>·duh·ruh <u>roo</u>·tuh <u>nay</u>·muhn
Can you drive *faster/slower*?	**Kunt u *sneller/langzamer* rijden?** kuhnt ew <u>snehl</u>·luhr/<u>lahng</u>·zaa·muhr <u>rie</u>·duhn

You May Hear…

Met welke luchtvaartmaatschappij vliegt u? meht <u>vehl</u>·kuh <u>luhkht</u>·faart·maat·skhah·<u>pie</u> fleekht ew — What airline are you flying?

Binnenlands of internationaal? <u>bih</u>·nuhn·lahnds ohf <u>ihn</u>·tuhr·naat·shoh·<u>naal</u> — Domestic or International?

Welke terminal? <u>vehl</u>·kuh <u>tuhr</u>·mee·nahl — What terminal?

You May See…

AANKOMST	arrivals
VERTREK	departures
BAGAGEAFHAALRUIMTE	baggage claim
BINNENLANDSE VLUCHTEN	domestic flights
INTERNATIONALE VLUCHTEN	international flights
INCHECKBALIE	check-in desk
E-TICKET INCHECKEN	e-ticket check-in
VERTREKGATES	departure gates

Check-in and Boarding

Where is check-in?	**Waar is de incheckbalie?** vaar ihs duh <u>ihn</u>·tshehk·<u>baa</u>·lee
My name is…	**Mijn naam is…** mien naam ihs…
I'm going to…	**Ik ga naar…** ihk khaa naar…
How much luggage is allowed?	**Hoeveel bagage is toegestaan?** <u>hoo</u>·fayl baa·<u>khaa</u>·zhuh ihs <u>too</u>·guh·staan
Which gate does flight…leave from?	**Van welke gate vertrekt vlucht…?** fahn <u>vehl</u>·kuh gayt fuhr·<u>trehkt</u> fluhkht…

I'd like *a window/ an aisle* seat.	**Ik wil graag een stoel *bij het raam/aan het gangpad.*** ihk vihl khraakh uhn stool *bie heht raam/aan heht khahng·paht*
When do we *leave/ arrive*?	**Wanneer *vertrekken/arriveren* we?** vah·nayr fuhr·trehk·kuhn/ahr·ree·vay·ruhn vuh
Is there any delay on flight…?	**Heeft vlucht…vertraging?** hayft fluhkht… fuhr·traa·khihng
How late will it be?	**Hoeveel vertraging heeft hij?** hoo·fayl fuhr·traa·khihng hayft hie

You May Hear…

De volgende! duh fohl·gun·duh	Next!
Uw *ticket/paspoort*, alstublieft. ew tih·kuht/ pahs·poart ahls·tew·bleeft	Your *ticket/passport*, please.
Hoeveel stuks bagage heeft u? hoo·fayl stuhks baa·khaa·zhuh hayft ew?	How many pieces of luggage do you have?
U heeft overbagage. ew hayft oa·fuhr·baa·khaa·zhuh	You have excess luggage.
Dat is te *zwaar/groot* voor handbagage. daht ihs tuh *zwaar/khroat* foar hahnt·baa·khaa·zhuh	That's too *heavy/ large* for a carry-on [to carry on board].
Heeft u deze tassen zelf ingepakt? hayft ew day·zuh tahs·suhn zehlf ihn·khuh·pahkt	Did you pack these bags yourself?
Heeft iemand iets aan u gegeven om mee te nemen? hayft ee·mahnd eets aan ew khuh·khay·fuhn ohm may tuh nay·muhn	Did anyone give you anything to carry?
Vlucht…is aan het boarden. fluhkht…ihs aan heht boar·duhn	Now boarding flight…

Luggage

Where *is/are*...?	**Waar *is/zijn*...?** vaar *ihs/zien*...
– the luggage carts [trolleys]	– **de bagagewagentjes** duh baa·<u>khaa</u>·zhuh·<u>vaa</u>·khuhn·tyuhs
– the luggage lockers	– **de bagagekluisjes** duh baa·<u>khaa</u>·zhuh·<u>klaws</u>·yuhs
– the baggage claim	– **de bagageafhaalruimte** duh baa·<u>khaa</u>·zhuh·<u>ahf</u>·haal·rawm·tuh
I've lost my luggage.	**Ik ben mijn bagage kwijtgeraakt.** ihk behn mien baa·<u>khaa</u>·zhuh <u>kviet</u>·khuh·raakt
My luggage has been stolen.	**Mijn bagage is gestolen.** mien baa·<u>khaa</u>·zhuh ihs khuh·<u>stoa</u>·luhn
My suitcase was damaged.	**Mijn koffer is beschadigd.** mien <u>kohf</u>·fuhr ihs buh·<u>skhaa</u>·dihkht

Finding Your Way

Where is...?	**Waar is...?** vaar ihs...
– the currency exchange office	– **het geldwisselkantoor** heht <u>khelt</u>·vihs·suhl·kahn·<u>toar</u>
– the car rental [hire]	– **het autoverhuurbedrijf** heht <u>ow</u>·toa·fuhr·<u>hewr</u>·buh·<u>drief</u>
– the exit	– **de uitgang** duh <u>awt</u>·khahng
– the taxi stand [rank]	– **de taxistandplaats** duh <u>tahk</u>·see·<u>stahnd</u>·plaats
Is there...Into town?	**Rijdt er...naar de stad?** riet ehr...naar duh staht
– a bus	– **een bus** uhn buhs
– a train	– **een trein** uhn trien
– a subway [underground]	– **een metro** uhn <u>may</u>·troa

▶ For directions, see page 33.

23

Train

How do I get to the train station?	**Hoe kom ik bij het station?** hoo kohm ihk bie heht staa·<u>shohn</u>
Is it far?	**Is het ver?** ihs heht fehr
Where *is/are...*?	**Waar *is/zijn...*?** vaar *ihs/zien...*
– the ticket office	**– het loket** heht loa·<u>keht</u>
– the luggage lockers	**– de bagagekluisjes** duh baa·<u>khaa</u>·zhuh·<u>klaws</u>·yuhs
– the platforms	**– de sporen** duh <u>spoa</u>·ruhn

▶ For directions, see page 33.

▶ For ticketing, see page 19.

You May See...

INFORMATIE	information
RESERVERINGEN	reservations
AANKOMST	arrivals
VERTREK	departures

24

Questions

Can I have a schedule [timetable]?	**Mag ik een spoorwegboekje?** mahkh ihk uhn spoar·vehkh·book·yuh
How long is the trip [journey]?	**Hoe lang duurt de reis?** hoo lahng dewrt duh ries
Do I have to change trains?	**Moet ik overstappen?** moot ihk oa·fuhr·stahp·puhn

> ***i*** **De Nederlandse Spoorwegen** (Netherlands Railways) offers three types of trains, which vary in how frequently they stop. Most stations are centrally located and you'll discover that the longest train trip within the Netherlands is only about three hours. There are two or more tracks to a platform, and electronic display signs will indicate which track a train will leave from.
>
> For domestic as well as international travel, a number of discounts are offered (group, children's, off-peak). Keep in mind that purchasing round-trip tickets, day travel cards or other specialty passes (Holland Rail, Summer Trip, Euro) is usually more economical than purchasing single tickets. Tickets may be purchased from machines or ticket offices in larger stations. There is a slight surcharge for tickets purchased at the counter. Note that you cannot buy tickets once on-board and you may be fined if you do not show a valid ticket.

Departures

Which platform does the train to...leave from?	**Van welk spoor vertrekt de trein naar...?** fahn vehlk spoar fuhr·trehkt duh trien naar...
Is this the right platform for...?	**Is dit het juiste spoor voor...?** ihs diht heht yaw·stuh spoar foar...
Where is platform...?	**Waar is spoor...?** vaar ihs spoar...

Where do I change for…?	**Waar stap ik over voor…?** vaar stahp ihk <u>oa</u>·fuhr foar

Boarding

Is this seat taken?	**Is deze plaats bezet?** ihs <u>day</u>·zuh plaats buh·<u>zeht</u>
That's my seat.	**Dat is mijn plaats.** daht ihs <u>mien</u> plaats

You May Hear…

Kaartjes, alstublieft. <u>kaart</u>·yuhs als·tew·<u>bleeft</u>	Tickets, please.
U moet overstappen in… ew moot <u>oa</u>·fuhr·stahp·puhn ihn…	You have to change at…
Volgende halte is… <u>fohl</u>·guhn·duh <u>hahl</u>·tuh ihs…	Next stop…

Bus

Where's the bus station?	**Waar is het busstation?** vaar ihs heht <u>buhs</u>·staa·<u>shohn</u>
How far is it?	**Hoe ver is het?** hoo fehr ihs heht
How do I get to…?	**Hoe kom ik in…?** hoo kohm ihk ihn…
Does the bus stop at…?	**Stopt de bus bij…?** stohpt duh buhs bie…
Can you tell me when to get off?	**Kunt u me waarschuwen wanneer ik moet uitstappen?** kuhnt ew muh <u>vaar</u>·skhew·vuhn <u>vah</u>·nayr ihk moot <u>awt</u>·stahp·puhn
Do I have to change buses?	**Moet ik overstappen?** moot ihk <u>oa</u>·fuhr·stahp·puhn
Can you stop here, please?	**Kunt u hier stoppen, alstublieft?** kuhnt ew heer <u>stohp</u>·puhn ahls·tew·<u>bleeft</u>

▶ For ticketing, see page 19.

For traveling short distances or for travel to destinations with no train service, taking the bus is a smart option. Service generally runs from around 6 a.m. until midnight.

There are two types of bus tickets of interest to visitors: the **strippenkaart** (strip ticket) and the **dagkaart** (day ticket). The strip ticket is divided into strips (sold in divisions of 2, 3, 8, 15 and 45), which are used up as you cross zones. You always need one more strip than the number of zones you plan to travel. You can either stamp the ticket yourself or have the driver do it. Stamps are valid for at least an hour, so you can transfer to other buses, subways or trams, as long as you stay within the same number of zones. The day ticket might be more economical if you plan on making a lot of trips in a single day.

For information on **excursies** (excursions) to classic tourist sights and for reservations, contact the **VVV, Vereniging voor Vreemdelingenverkeer** (tourist information office).

You May See...

BUSHALTE	bus stop
INGANG/UITGANG	enter/exit
KAARTJE STEMPELEN	stamp your ticket

Subway [Underground]

Where's the nearest subway [underground] station? **Waar is het dichtstbijzijnde metrostation?** vaar ihs heht dihkhtst·bie·zien·duh may·troa·staa·<u>shohn</u>

Can I have a map of the subway [underground]? **Mag ik een kaart van de metro?** mahkh ihk uhn kaart fahn duh <u>may</u>·troa

Which line for…?	**Welke lijn gaat naar…?** <u>vehl</u>·kuh lien khaat naar…
Where do I change for…?	**Waar stap ik over voor…?** vaar stahp ihk <u>oa</u>·fuhr foar…
Is this the right train for…?	**Is dit de juiste trein naar…?** ihs diht duh <u>yaw</u>·stuh trien naar…
Where are we?	**Waar zijn we?** vaar zien vuh

▶ For ticketing, see page 19.

Subway service is an option from around 6 a.m. to midnight in and around Amsterdam and Rotterdam. You can use the **strippenkaart** (strip ticket) or buy a ticket from the automatic ticket machines. For the strip ticket, remember that you will always need one more strip than the number of zones you are going to travel. In Amsterdam, you also have the option of purchasing a **dagkaart** (day ticket), which offers unlimited travel on trams, buses, subways and canal buses.

Boat and Ferry

| When is the ferry to…? | **Wanneer vertrekt de veerboot naar…?** <u>vah</u>·nayr fuhr·<u>trehkt</u> duh <u>fayr</u>·boat naar… |
| Can I take my car? | **Kan ik mijn auto meenemen?** kahn ihk mien <u>ow</u>·toa <u>may</u>·nay·muhn |

▶ For ticketing, see page 19.

You May See…

| **REDDINGSBOTEN** | life boats |
| **REDDINGSVESTEN** | life jackets |

There are a number of ferry companies with service to and from the Netherlands. Stena Line offers up to four sailings daily between **Hoek van Holland** (Hook of Holland) and Harwich, U.K. P&O Ferries sails between Rotterdam and Hull, U.K., while DFDS Seaways provides service from the Port of Ijmuiden in Amsterdam to Newcastle, U.K., up to seven times a week.

Inland ferries can also be taken to travel to **Waddeneilanden** (Frisian Islands), across **IJsselmeer** (IJssel Lake) and on many small rivers.

Another option for water travel in Amsterdam is the canal bus; it offers regular service and stops that are located near the major museums, attractions and shopping areas. A **dagkaart** (day ticket) allows you to hop on and off as many times as you like until noon the next day. With this ticket you may also transfer to the subway free of charge.

Bicycle and Motorcycle

I'd like to rent [hire]…	**Ik wil graag een…huren.** ihk vihl khraakh uhn…<u>hew</u>·ruhn
– a bicycle	**– fiets** feets
– a moped	**– brommer** <u>brohm</u>·muhr
– a motorcycle	**– motorfiets** <u>moa</u>·tuhr·feets
How much per *day/week*?	**Hoeveel kost het per *dag/week*?** <u>hoo</u>·fayl kohst heht pehr *dahkh/vayk*
Can I have a *helmet/lock*?	**Mag ik een *helm/slot*?** Mahkh ihk uhn *hehlm/sloht*

Cycling is very much a part of daily life in the Netherlands. Paths are marked with red and white signs or blue signs with a white bicycle for obligatory separate bike lanes.

Bikes may be rented at more than 100 train stations in the Netherlands. The daily rate is quite cheap, though you may have to leave a relatively high deposit. This will be returned when you bring the bike back in good condition.

You can take your bike on the train. There are a few things to remember though. You must purchase a ticket for your bike. It must travel in the special bike compartment. And you are not allowed to travel with bikes during rush hour.

Taxi

Where can I get a taxi?	**Waar kan ik een taxi krijgen?** vaar kahn ihk uhn <u>tahk</u>·see <u>krie</u>·khuhn
I'd like a taxi for tomorrow at…	**Ik wil graag een taxi voor morgen om… uur.** ihk vihl khraakh uhn <u>tahk</u>·see foar <u>mohr</u>·khuhn ohm…ewr
Pick me up at…	**Haal me op om…** haal muh ohp ohm…
Can you take me to…?	**Kunt u me naar…brengen?** kuhnt ew muh naar…<u>brehng</u>·uhn
– this address	**– dit adres** diht ah·<u>drehs</u>
– the airport	**– het vliegveld** heht <u>fleekh</u>·fehlt
– the train station	**– het station** heht staa·<u>shohn</u>
I'm in a hurry.	**Ik heb haast.** ihk hehp haast
Can you drive *faster/ slower*?	**Kunt u *sneller/langzamer* rijden?** kuhnt ew <u>snehl</u>·luhr/<u>lahng</u>·zaa·muhr <u>rie</u>·duhn
Stop/Wait here.	***Stop/Wacht* hier.** stohp/vahkht heer
How much?	**Hoeveel kost het?** <u>hoo</u>·fayl kohst heht
You said…euros.	**U zei…euro.** ew zie…<u>u</u>·roa

Keep the change.	**Houdt u het wisselgeld maar.** howt ew heht <u>vihs</u>·suhl·khehlt maar

▶For numbers, see page 158.

You May Hear...

Waar naartoe? vaar naar too	Where to?
Welk adres? vehlk ah·<u>drehs</u>	What's the address?

Dutch taxis are marked by blue license plates and the word **TAXI** on the roof. Taxis should usually be booked in advance, rather than hailed in the street, though you might be able to hail one in larger cities. You can also go to a **taxistandplaats** (taxi stand). Tip by rounding up the fare.

There are also water taxis on the canals in Amsterdam.

Car

Car Rental [Hire]

Where can I rent a car?	**Waar kan ik een auto huren?** vaar kahn ihk uhn <u>ow</u>·toa <u>hew</u>·ruhn
I'd like to rent [hire]...	**Ik wil graag...huren.** Ihk vihl khraakh...<u>hew</u>·ruhn
– an automatic	**– een automaat** uhn ow·toa·<u>maat</u>
– a car with air conditioning	**– een auto met airco** uhn <u>ow</u>·toa meht <u>air</u>·coa
– a car seat	**– een kinderzitje** uhn <u>kihn</u>·duhr·ziht·yuh
How much...?	**Hoeveel kost het...?** <u>hoo</u>·fayl kohst heht...
– per *day/week*	**– per *dag/week*** pehr *dahkh/vayk*
– per kilometer	**– per kilometer** pehr <u>kee</u>·loa·may·tuhr
– for unlimited mileage	**– met onbeperkt aantal kilometers** meht ohn·buh·<u>pehrkt</u> <u>aan</u>·tahl <u>kee</u>·loa·may·tuhrs
– with insurance	**– met verzekering** meht fuhr·<u>zay</u>·kuh·rihng

| Are there any discounts for...? | **Zijn er ook kortingen voor...?** zien ehr oak kohr·tihng·uhn foar... |

You May Hear...

Heeft u een internationaal rijbewijs? hayft ew uhn ihn·tuhr·naat·shoo·naal rie·buh·wies	Do you have an international driver's license?
Mag ik uw paspoort zien, alstublieft? mahkh ihk ew pahs·poart zeen ahls·tew·bleeft	Your passport, please.
Wilt u extra verzekering? vihlt ew ehk·straa fuhr·zay·kuh·rihng	Do you want insurance?
U moet een borgsom betalen van... ew moot uhn bohrkh·sohm buh·taa·luhn fahn...	There is a deposit of...
Kunt u hier even tekenen? kuhnt ew heer ay·fuhn tay·kuh·nuhn	Can you sign here?

Gas [Petrol] Station

Where's the next gas [petrol] station?	**Waar is het volgende benzinestation?** vaar ihs heht fohl·khuhn·duh behn·zee·nuh·staa·shohn
Fill it up, please.	**Vol, alstublieft.** fohl ahls·tew·bleeft
...liters, please.	**...liter, alstublieft.** ...lee·tuhr ahls·tew·bleeft
I'd like to pay *in cash/ by credit card*.	**Ik wil graag *contant/met een creditcard* betalen.** ihk vihl khraakh *kohn·tahnt/meht uhn kreh·diht·kaart* buh·taa·luhn

You May See...

NORMAAL	regular
SUPER	premium [super]
DIESEL	diesel

Asking Directions

Is this the right road to…?	**Is dit de juiste weg naar…?** ihs diht duh yaw·stuh vehkh naar…
How far is it to… from here?	**Hoe ver is het hiervandaan naar…?** hoo fehr ihs heht heer·fahn·daan naar…
Where's…?	**Waar vind ik…?** vaar fihnt ihk…
– …Street	**– de…straat** duh…straat
– this address	**– dit adres** diht ah·drehs
– the highway [motorway]	**– de snelweg** duh snehl·vehkh
Can you show me on the map?	**Kunt u dat op de kaart laten zien?** kuhnt ew daht ohp duh kaart laa·tuhn zeen
I'm lost.	**Ik ben verdwaald.** ihk behn fuhr·dwaalt

You May Hear...

rechtdoor rehkht·doar	straight ahead
links lihnks	left
rechts rehkhts	right
op/om **de hoek** *ohp/ohm* duh hook	*on/around* the corner
tegenover tay·khuhn·oa·fuhr	opposite
achter ahkh·tuhr	behind
naast naast	next to
na naa	after
ten noorden/ten zuiden tehn noar·duhn/tehn zaw·duhn	north/south
ten oosten/ten westen tehn oas·tuhn/tehn vehs·tuhn	east/west

You May See...

🛑	**STOP**	stop
▽	**VOORRANG VERLENEN**	yield
⊗	**VERBODEN STIL TE STAAN**	no standing
⊘	**VERBODEN TE PARKEREN**	no parking
←	**EENRICHTINGSVERKEER**	one way
⊖	**VERBODEN IN TE RIJDEN**	no entry
🚗	**VERBODEN IN TE HALEN**	no passing
↩	**VERBODEN TE KEREN**	no U-turn
↱	**AFSLAG**	exit
🚸	**VOETGANGERSOVERSTEEKPLAATS**	pedestrian crossing

Parking

Can I park here?	**Mag ik hier parkeren?** mahkh ihk heer pahr·<u>kay</u>·ruhn
Is there a parking lot [car park] nearby?	**Is er een parkeergarage in de buurt?** ihs ehr uhn pahr·<u>kayr</u>·khaa·<u>raa</u>·zhuh ihn duh bewrt
How much...?	**Hoeveel kost het...?** <u>hoo</u>·fayl kohst heht...
– per hour	**– per uur** pehr ewr

| – per day | **– per dag** pehr dahkh |
| – overnight | **– per nacht** pehr nahkht |

Breakdown and Repairs

My car broke down.	**Ik heb autopech.** ihk hehp <u>ow</u>·toa·pehkh
My car won't start.	**Mijn auto wil niet starten.** mien <u>ow</u>·toa vihl neet <u>stahr</u>·tuhn
Can you fix it?	**Kunt u hem repareren?** kuhnt ew hehm <u>ray</u>·paa·<u>ray</u>·ruhn
When will it be ready?	**Wanneer is hij klaar?** <u>vahn</u>·nayr ihs hie klaar
How much?	**Hoeveel kost het?** <u>hoo</u>·fayl kohst heht

Accidents

| There's been an accident. | **Er is een ongeluk gebeurd.** ehr ihs uhn <u>ohn</u>·khuh·luhk khuh·<u>burt</u> |
| Call *an ambulance/ the police.* | **Bel *een ambulance/de politie.*** bel *uhn ahm·bew·<u>lahn</u>·suh/duh poa·<u>leet</u>·see* |

Accommodations

Essential

Can you recommend a hotel?	**Kunt u een hotel aanbevelen?** kuhnt ew uhn hoa·<u>tehl</u> <u>aan</u>·buh·fay·luhn
I have a reservation.	**Ik heb een reservering.** ihk hehp uhn <u>ray</u>·zuhr·<u>vay</u>·rihng
My name is…	**Mijn naam is…** mien naam ihs…
Do you have a room…?	**Heeft u een kamer…?** hayft ew uhn <u>kaa</u>·muhr…
– for one	**– voor één persoon** foar ayn puhr·<u>soan</u>

Do you have a room…?	**Heeft u een kamer…?** hayft ew uhn <u>kaa</u>·muhr…
– for two	**– voor twee personen** foar tvay puhr·<u>soa</u>·nuhn
– with a *bathroom [toilet]/shower*	**– met *toilet/douche*** meht twaa·<u>leht</u>/doosh
– with air conditioning	**– met airco** meht <u>air</u>·coa
For tonight.	**Voor vannacht.** foar fahn·<u>nahkht</u>
For two nights.	**Voor twee nachten.** foar tvay <u>nahkh</u>·tuhn
For one week.	**Voor één week.** foar ayn vayk
How much?	**Hoeveel kost het?** <u>hoo</u>·fayl kohst heht
Do you have anything cheaper?	**Heeft u iets goedkopers?** hayft ew eets khoot·<u>koa</u>·puhrs
When's check-out?	**Hoe laat moeten we uitchecken?** hoo laat <u>moo</u>·tuhn vie <u>awt</u>·check·uhn
Can I leave this in the safe?	**Mag ik dit in de kluis bewaren?** mahkh ihk diht ihn duh klaws buh·<u>waa</u>·ruhn
Can we leave our bags?	**Mogen we onze bagage hier laten staan?** <u>moa</u>·khuhn wie <u>ohn</u>·zuh baa·<u>khaa</u>·zhuh heer <u>laa</u>·tuhn staan
Can I have *the bill/ a receipt*?	**Mag ik *de rekening/een kwitantie*?** mahkh ihk duh <u>ray</u>·kuh·nihng/uhn <u>kvee</u>·tahnt·see
I'll pay *in cash/by credit card*.	**Ik wil graag *contant/met een creditcard* betalen.** ihk vihl khraakh kohn·<u>tahnt</u>/meht uhn <u>kreh</u>·diht·kaart buh·<u>taa</u>·luhn

If you didn't reserve a room before your arrival, visit the local **VVV**, **Vereniging voor Vreemdelingenverkeer** (tourist information office). There you can find recommendations on hotels and arrange reservations for a small fee.

Finding Lodging

Can you recommend a hotel?	**Kunt u een hotel aanbevelen?** kuhnt ew uhn hoa·<u>tehl</u> <u>aan</u>·buh·fay·luhn
What is it near?	**Waar ligt het bij in de buurt?** vaar lihkht heht bie lhn duh bewrt
How do I get there?	**Hoe kom ik er?** hoo kohm ihk ehr

In the Netherlands, there are a variety of accommodation options in addition to hotels, which range from one to five stars. You could choose to stay in a bed and breakfast, a **motel** (motel) if you are traveling by car, a **jeugdherberg** (youth hostel) or in a **vakantiehuisje** (vacation house). **Vakantiehuisje** refers to any rented living space, such as vacation cottages, apartments or houseboats. You might also want to try one of the **Centre Parcs**, which are vacation villages.

Prices are generally given per room and include breakfast, service charges and taxes (but do not include the extra city tax in Amsterdam). Reservations can be made through the Netherlands Reservation Center, which is free, **VVV** tourist offices, which charge a fee, and **GWK** (**Grenswisselkantoren**) offices.

At the Hotel

I have a reservation.	**Ik heb een reservering.** ihk hehp uhn <u>ray</u>·zuhr·<u>vay</u>·rihng
My name is…	**Mijn naam is…** mien naam ihs…
Do you have a room…?	**Heeft u een kamer…?** hayft ew uhn <u>kaa</u>·muhr…
– with a *bathroom [toilet]/shower*	**– met *toilet/douche*** meht *twaa·<u>leht</u>/doosh*
– with air conditioning	**– met airco** meht <u>air</u>·coa
– that's *smoking/ non-smoking*	**– voor *rokers/niet-rokers*** foar *<u>roa</u>·kuhrs/neet·<u>roa</u>·kuhrs*
Does the hotel have…?	**Heeft het hotel…?** hayft heht hoa·<u>tehl</u>…
– a computer	**– een computer** uhn kohm·<u>pyoo</u>·tuhr
– an elevator [lift]	**– een lift** uhn lihft
– (wireless) internet service	**– (draadloze) internetverbinding** (<u>draat</u>·loa·zuh) <u>ihn</u>·tuhr·neht·fuhr·<u>bihn</u>·dihng
– room service	**– roomservice** <u>room</u>·suhr·vihs
– a gym	**– een fitnessruimte** uhn <u>fiht</u>·nehs·<u>rawm</u>·tuh
I need…	**Ik wil…** ihk vihl…
– an extra bed	**– een extra bed** uhn <u>ehk</u>·straa beht
– a cot	**– een kinderbed** uhn <u>kihn</u>·duhr·beht
– a crib [child's cot]	**– een wieg** uhn veekh

You May Hear…

Uw *paspoort/creditcard*, alstublieft.	Your *passport/credit card*, please.
Kunt u dit hier tekenen?	Can you sign here?

Price

How much per *night/ week*?
Hoeveel kost het per *nacht/week*?
<u>hoo</u>·fayl kohst heht pehr *nahkht/vayk*

Does the price include *breakfast/sales tax [VAT]*?
Is *het ontbijt/de BTW* bij de prijs inbegrepen? Ihs heht ohnt·<u>biet</u>/bay·tay·<u>vay</u> bie duh pries ihn·buh·<u>khray</u>·puhn

Questions

Where's…? **Waar is…?** vaar ihs…

– the bar **– de bar** duh bahr

– the bathroom [toilet] **– het toilet** heht tvaa·<u>leht</u>

– the elevator [lift] **– de lift** duh lihft

Can I have…? **Mag ik…?** mahkh ihk…

– a blanket **– een deken** uhn <u>day</u>·kuhn

– an iron **– een strijkijzer** uhn <u>striek</u>·ie·zuhr

– a pillow **– een kussen** uhn <u>kuh</u>·suhn

– soap **– zeep** zayp

– toilet paper **– toiletpapier** tvaa·<u>leht</u>·paa·peer

– a towel **– een handdoek** uhn <u>hahn</u>·dook

Do you have an adapter for this?
Heeft u hier een adapter voor? hayft ew heer uhn ah·<u>dahp</u>·tuhr foar

How do I turn on the lights?
Hoe doe ik het licht aan? hoo doo ihk heht lihkht aan

Can you wake me at…?
Kunt u me om…wakker maken? kuhnt ew muh ohm…<u>vahk</u>·kuhr <u>maa</u>·kuhn

Can I have my things from the safe?
Mag ik mijn spullen uit de kluis hebben? mahkh ihk mien <u>spuh</u>·luhn awt duh klaws <u>heh</u>·buhn

Are there any messages for me?
Zijn er berichten voor me? zien ehr buh·<u>rihkh</u>·tuhn foar muh

You May See...

DUWEN/TREKKEN	push/pull
TOILET	restroom [toilet]
DOUCHE	shower
LIFT	elevator [lift]
TRAP	stairs
WASSERIJ	laundry
NIET STOREN	do not disturb
NOODUITGANG/BRANDTRAP	*emergency/fire exit*
WEKDIENST	wake-up call

Problems

There's a problem.	**Ik heb een probleem.** ihk hehp uhn <u>proa</u>·blaym
I've lost my *key/key card.*	**Ik heb mijn *sleutel/sleutelkaart* verloren.** ihk hehp mien <u>slu</u>·tuhl/<u>slu</u>·tuhl·kaart fuhr·<u>loa</u>·ruhn
I've locked myself out of my room.	**Ik heb mezelf buitengesloten.** ihk hehp muh·<u>zehlf</u> <u>baw</u>·tuhn·khuh·<u>sloa</u>·tuhn
There's no *hot water/ toilet paper.*	**Er is geen *warm water/toiletpapier.*** ehr ihs khayn *vahrm <u>vaa</u>·tuhr/tvaa·<u>leht</u>·paa·peer*
The room is dirty.	**De kamer is vies.** duh <u>kaa</u>·muhr ihs vees
There are bugs in our room.	**Er zijn insecten op onze kamer.** ehr zien ihn·<u>sehk</u>·tuhn ohp <u>ohn</u>·zuh <u>kaa</u>·muhr
...doesn't work.	**...doet het niet.** ...doot heht neet
Can you fix...?	**Kunt u...repareren?** kuhnt ew... <u>ray</u>·paa·<u>ray</u>·ruhn

– the air conditioning	**– de airco** duh <u>air</u>·coa
– the fan	**– de ventilator** duh <u>fehn</u>·tee·<u>laa</u>·tohr
– the heat [heating]	**– de verwarming** duh fehr·<u>vahr</u>·mihng
– the light	**– het licht** heht lihkht
– the TV	**– de tv** duh tay·<u>vay</u>
– the toilet	**– het toilet** heht tvaa·<u>leht</u>
I'd like to move to another room.	**Ik wil graag een andere kamer.** ihk vihl khraakh uhn <u>ahn</u>·duh·ruh <u>kaa</u>·muhr

Electricity in the Netherlands is 220 volts and sockets are for two-pin plugs. British and American appliances will need an adapter.

Check-out

When's check-out?	**Hoe laat moeten we uitchecken?** hoo laat <u>moo</u>·tuhn vie <u>awt</u>·tshehk·kuhn
Can I leave my bags here until…?	**Mag ik mijn bagage hier laten staan tot…?** mahkh ihk mien baa·<u>khaa</u>·zhuh heer <u>laa</u>·tuhn staan toht…
Can I have an *itemized bill/a receipt*?	**Mag ik een *gespecificeerde rekening/ kwitantie*?** mahkh ihk uhn khuh·<u>spay</u>·see·fee·<u>sayr</u>·duh <u>ray</u>·kuh·nihng/ kvee·<u>tahnt</u>·see
I think there's a mistake in this bill.	**Ik geloof dat deze rekening niet klopt.** ihk khuh·<u>loaf</u> daht <u>day</u>·zuh <u>ray</u>·kuh·nihng neet klohpt
I'll pay *in cash/by credit card*.	**Ik wil graag *contant/met een creditcard* betalen.** ihk vihl khraakh *kohn·<u>tahnt</u>/meht uhn <u>kreh</u>·diht·kaart* buh·<u>taa</u>·luhn

Renting ───────────────────

I've reserved *an apartment/a room*.	**Ik heb *een appartement/kamer* gereserveerd.** lhk hehp uhn *ah·pahr·tuh·mehnt/kaa·muhr* khuh·ray·zuhr·fayrt
My name is…	**Mijn naam is…** mien naam ihs…
Can I have the *key/key card*?	**Mag ik de *sleutel/sleutelkaart*?** mahkh ihk duh *slu·tuhl/slu·tuhl·kaart*
Do you have…?	**Heeft u…?** hayft ew…
– dishes	**– serviesgoed** sehr·vees·khoot
– pillows	**– kussens** kuh·suhns
– sheets	**– lakens** laa·kuhns
– towels	**– handdoeken** hahn·doo·kuhn
When/Where do I put out the trash [rubbish]?	***Wanneer/Waar* moet ik de vuilnis buiten zetten?** *vah·nayr/vaar* moot ihk duh vawl·nihs baw·tuhn zeht·tuhn
…is broken.	**…is kapot.** …ihs kaa·poht
How does…work?	**Hoe werkt…?** hoo vehrkt…
– the air conditioner	**– de airco** duh air·coa
– the dishwasher	**– de afwasmachine** duh ahf·vahs·maa·shee·nuh
– the freezer	**– de diepvriezer** duh deep·free·zuhr
– the heater	**– de verwarming** duh fuhr·vahr·mihng
– the microwave	**– de magnetron** duh mahkh·nuh·trohn
– the refrigerator	**– de koelkast** duh kool·kahst
– the stove	**– het fornuis** heht fohr·naws
– the washing machine	**– de wasmachine** duh vahs·maa·shee·nuh

Household Items

I need...	**Ik heb...nodig.** ihk hehp...noa·dihkh
– an adapter	**– een adapter** uhn aa·dahp·tuhr
– aluminum [kitchen] foil	**– aluminiumfolie** aa·loo·mee·nee·yuhm·foa·lee
– a bottle opener	**– een flesopener** uhn flehs·oa·puh·nuhr
– a broom	**– een bezem** uhn bay·zuhm
– a can opener	**– een blikopener** uhn blihk·oa·puh·nuhr
– cleaning supplies	**– schoonmaakmiddelen** skhoan·maak·mih·duh·luhn
– a corkscrew	**– een kurkentrekker** uhn kuhr·kuhn·trehk·kuhr
– detergent	**– waspoeder** vahs·poo·duhr
– dishwashing liquid	**– afwasmiddel** ahf·vahs·mih·duhl
– garbage [rubbish] bags	**– vuilniszakken** fawl·nihs·zah·kuhn
– a light bulb	**– een gloeilamp** uhn khlooy·lahmp
– matches	**= lucifers** lew·sih·fehrs
– a mop	**– een dweil** uhn dwiel
– napkins	**– servetten** sehr·feh·tuhn
– paper towels	**– keukenpapier** ku·kuhn·paa·peer
– plastic wrap [cling film]	**– huishoudfolie** haws·hout·foa·lee
– a plunger	**– een ontstopper** uhn ohnt·stoh·puhr
– scissors	**– een schaar** uhn skhaar
– a vacuum cleaner	**– een stofzuiger** uhn stohf·zaw·khurh

▶ For dishes and utensils, see page 62.

▶ For oven temperatures, see page 164.

Hostel

Do you have any places left for tonight?	**Heeft u nog plaatsen vrij voor vannacht?** hayft ew nohkh <u>plaat</u>·suhn frie foar fahn·<u>nahkht</u>
Can I have...?	**Mag ik...?** mahkh ihk...
– a blanket	**– een deken** uhn <u>day</u>·kuhn
– a pillow	**– een kussen** uhn <u>kuh</u>·suhn
– soap	**– zeep** zayp
– towels	**– handdoeken** <u>hahn</u>·doo·kuhn
What time do you lock up?	**Hoe laat sluit u?** hoo laat slawt ew

i
Known as **Stayokay**, the Dutch Youth Hostel Association operates some 30 official youth hostels around the Netherlands in buildings ranging from modern facilities to castles or country houses. You may request a private or shared room; breakfast and sheets are included in the price. Hostelling International (HI) cardholders are exempt from surcharges and receive special discounts. You may purchase HI cards on the spot.

There are also a number of unofficial hostels throughout the country. The quality of these may range from poor to excellent.

Camping

Can we camp here?	**Mogen we hier kamperen?** <u>moa</u>·khuhn vie heer kahm·<u>pay</u>·ruhn
Is there a campsite near here?	**Is er een camping in de buurt?** ihs ehr uhn <u>kehm</u>·pihng ihn duh bewrt
What is the charge per *day/week*?	**Hoeveel kost het per *dag/week*?** <u>hoo</u>·fayl kohst heht pehr *daakh/vayk*

Do you have…?	**Heeft u…?** hayft ew…
– cooking facilities	**– kookgelegenheid** <u>koak</u>·khuh·<u>lay</u>·khuhn·hiet
– electrical outlets	**– stopcontacten** <u>stohp</u>·kohn·tahk·tuhn
– laundry facilities	**– wasmachines** <u>vahs</u>·maa·shee·nuhs
– showers	**– douches** <u>doo</u>·shuhs
– tents for rent [hire]	**– tenten te huur** <u>tehn</u>·tuhn tuh hewr
Where can I empty the chemical toilet?	**Waar kan ik het chemisch toilet legen?** vaar kahn ihk heht <u>khay</u>·mees tvaa·<u>leht</u> <u>lay</u>·khun

You May See…

DRINKWATER	drinking water
VERBODEN TE KAMPEREN	no camping
GEEN *KAMPVUREN/BARBECUES*	no *fires/barbecues*

▶ For household items, see page 43.

▶ For dishes, utensils and kitchen tools, see page 62.

Internet and Communications

Essential

Where's an internet cafe?	**Waar vind ik een internetcafé?** vaar fihnt ihk uhn <u>ihn</u>·tuhr·neht·kaa·<u>fay</u>
Can I *access the internet/check e-mail* here?	**Kan ik hier *internetten/mijn e-mail checken*?** kahn ihk heer <u>ihn</u>·tuhr·neh·tuhn/ mien <u>ee</u>·mayl <u>tsheh</u>·kuhn
How much per *hour/ half hour*?	**Hoeveel kost het per *uur/half uur*?** <u>hoo</u>·fayl kohst heht pehr *ewr/hahlf ewr*

How do I *connect/ log on*?	**Hoe kan ik *verbinding maken/ inloggen*?** hoo kahn ihk *fuhr-bihn-dihng maa-kuhn/ihn-loh-khun*
I'd like a phone card, please.	**Ik wil een telefoonkaart, alstublieft.** ihk vihl uhn tay-luh-foan-kaart ahls-tew-bleeft
Can I have your phone number?	**Mag ik uw telefoonnummer?** mahkh ihk ew tay-luh-foan-nuh-muhr
Here's my *number/ e-mail address*.	**Hier is mijn *telefoonnummer/ e-mailadres*.** heer ihs mien *tay-luh-foan-nuh-muhr/ee-mayl-aa-drehs*
Call me.	**Bel me.** behl muh
E-mail me.	**Stuur me een e-mail.** stewr muh uhn ee-mayl
Hello. This is…	**Dag. U spreekt met…** daakh ew spraykt meht…
I'd like to speak to…	**Ik wil graag met…spreken.** ihk vihl khraakh meht…spray-kuhn
Can you repeat that?	**Kunt u dat herhalen?** kuhnt ew daht hehr-haa-luhn
I'll call back later.	**Ik bel straks wel even terug.** ihk behl strahks vehl ay-fuhn truhkh
Bye.	**Dag.** dahkh
Where's the post office?	**Waar is het postkantoor?** vaar ihs heht pohst-kahn-toar
I'd like to send this to…	**Ik wil dit versturen naar…** ihk vihl diht fuhr-stew-ruhn naar…

Computer, Internet and E-mail

| Where's an internet cafe? | **Waar vind ik een internetcafé?** vaar fihnt ihk uhn ihn-tuhr-neht-kaa-fay |
| Does it have wireless internet? | **Is er draadloos internet?** ihs ehr draat-loas ihn-tuhr-neht |

How do I turn the computer *on/off*?	**Hoe zet ik de computer *aan/uit?*** hoo zeht ihk duh kohm·<u>pyoo</u>·tuhr *aan/awt*
Can I...?	**Kan ik...?** kahn ihk...
– access the internet here	**– hier internetten** heer <u>ihn</u>·tuhr·neh·tuhn
– check e-mail	**– mijn e-mail checken** mien <u>ee</u>·mayl <u>tsheh</u>·kuhn
– print	**– printen** <u>prihn</u>·tuhn
How much per *hour/ half hour*?	**Hoeveel kost het per *uur/half uur?*** <u>hoo</u>·fayl kohst heht pehr *ewr/hahlf ewr*
How do I...?	**Hoe moet ik...?** hoo moot ihk...
– connect/disconnect	**– verbinding maken/de verbinding verbreken** fuhr·<u>bihn</u>·dihng <u>maa</u>·kuhn/duh fuhr·<u>bihn</u>·dihng fuhr·<u>bray</u>·kuhn
– log *on/off*	**– inloggen/uitloggen** <u>ihn</u>·lohkh·uhn/ <u>awt</u>·lohkh·uhn
– type this symbol	**– dit symbool typen** diht sihm·<u>boal</u> <u>tee</u>·puhn
What's your e-mail?	**Wat is uw e-mailadres?** vaht ihs ew <u>ee</u>·mayl·aa·<u>drehs</u>
My e-mail is...	**Mijn e-mailadres is...** mien <u>ee</u>·mayl·aa·<u>drehs</u> ihs...

You May See...

E-MAIL	e-mail
AFSLUITEN	exit
HELP	help
INSTANT MESSENGER	instant messenger
INTERNET	internet
INLOGGEN	login
AAN/UIT	on/off
AFDRUKKEN	print
VERZENDEN	send
GEBRUIKERSNAAM/WACHTWOORD	username/password
DRAADLOOS INTERNET	wireless internet

Phone

A phone card, please.	**Een telefoonkaart, alstublieft.** uhn tay·luh·<u>foan</u>·kaart ahls·tew·<u>bleeft</u>
How much?	**Hoeveel kost het?** <u>hoo</u>·fayl kohst heht
My phone doesn't work here.	**Mijn telefoon werkt hier niet.** mien tay·luh·<u>foan</u> vehrkt heer neet
What's the *area/ country* code for...?	**Wat is het *netnummer/landnummer* van...?** vaht ihs heht <u>neht</u>·nuh·muhr/<u>lahnt</u>·nuh·muhr fahn...
What's the number for Information?	**Wat is het nummer van Inlichtingen?** vaht ihs heht <u>nuh</u>·muhr fahn <u>ihn</u>·likh·tihng·uhn
I'd like the number for...	**Ik zoek het nummer van...** ihk zook heht <u>nuh</u>·muhr fahn...

| Can I have your number? | **Mag ik uw nummer?** mahkh ihk ew <u>nuh</u>·muhr |
| Can I have your number? | **Mag ik uw nummer?** mahkh ihk ew nuh·muhr |

Can I have your number? | **Mag ik uw nummer?** mahkh ihk ew <u>nuh</u>·muhr

My number is... | **Mijn nummer is...** mien <u>nuh</u>·muhr is...

▶ For numbers, see page 158.

Please call me. | **Ik verzoek u me te bellen.** ihk fuhr·<u>zook</u> ew muh tuh <u>beh</u>·luhn

Please text me. | **Ik verzoek u me te sms'en.** ihk fuhr·<u>zook</u> ew muh tuh <u>ehs</u>·ehm·<u>ehs</u>·uhn

I'll call you. | **Ik zal u bellen.** ihk zahl ew <u>beh</u>·luhn

I'll text you. | **Ik zal u sms'en.** ihk zahl ew <u>ehs</u>·ehm·<u>ehs</u>·uhn

On the Phone

Hello. This is... | **Dag. U spreekt met...** dahkh ew spraykt meht...

I'd like to speak to... | **Ik wil graag met...spreken.** ihk vihl khraakh meht...<u>spray</u>·kuhn

Extension... | **Toestel...** <u>too</u>·stehl...

Can you speak *louder/ more slowly*? | **Kunt u iets *harder/langzamer* spreken?** kuhnt ew eets *<u>hahr</u>·duhr/ <u>lahng</u>·zaa·muhr* <u>spray</u>·kuhn

Can you repeat that?	**Kunt u dat herhalen?** kuhnt ew daht hehr·<u>haa</u>·luhn
I'll call back later.	**Ik bel straks wel even terug.** ihk behl strahks vehl <u>ay</u>·fuhn truhkh
Bye.	**Dag.** dahkh

▶For business travel, see page 137.

You May Hear...

Met wie spreek ik? meht vee sprayk ihk	Who's calling?
Kunt u aan de lijn blijven? kuhnt ew aan duh lien <u>blie</u>·fuhn	Hold on.
Hij♂/Zij♀ is niet beschikbaar. hie♂/zie♀ ihs neet buh·<u>skhihk</u>·baar	He/She can't come to the phone.
Wilt u een bericht achterlaten? vihlt ew uhn buh·<u>rikht</u> ahkh·tuhr·<u>laa</u>·tuhn	Would you like to leave a message?
Kan hij♂/zij♀ u terugbellen? kahn hie♂/zie♀ ew <u>truhkh</u>·beh·luhn	Can he/she call you back?
Wat is uw nummer? vaht ihs ew <u>nuh</u>·muhr	What's your number?

Fax

Can I *send/receive* a fax here?	**Kan ik hier een fax *versturen/ontvangen?*** kahn ihk heer uhn fahks fuhr·<u>stew</u>·ruhn/ohnt·<u>fahng</u>·uhn
What's the fax number?	**Wat is het faxnummer?** vaht ihs heht <u>fahks</u>·nuh·muhr
Please fax this to…	**Kunt u dit faxen naar…** kuhnt ew diht <u>fahk</u>·suhn naar…

i Public phones, mainly found in and around most train stations, are disappearing in the Netherlands due to the popularity of mobile phones. Public phones accept credit cards and **Telfort** phone cards, which may be purchased at all **NS** station ticket offices as well from **GWK** and some shops. Many public phones no longer accept coins. Schiphol Airport has added a new type of public phone, the **Multifoon** (multi-phone), which is a telecommunications pillar that can be used to make calls, send e-mail and request information via the internet.

Important telephone numbers:
emergencies, 112
operator assistance, 0800 0410

To call the U.S. or Canada from the Netherlands or Belgium, dial 00 + 1 + area code + phone number. To call the U.K., dial 00 + 44 + area code (minus the first 0) + phone number.

Post Office

Where's the *post office/mailbox [postbox]*?	**Waar is *het postkantoor/de brievenbus*?** vaar ihs *heht pohst·kahn·toar/duh bree·fuhn·buhs*
A stamp for this *letter/ postcard*, please.	**Een postzegel voor deze *brief/ansichtkaart*, alstublieft.** uhn pohst·zay·khuhl foar day·zuh *breef/ahn·sihkht·kaart* ahls·tew·bleeft
How much?	**Hoeveel kost het?** hoo·fayl kohst heht
I want to send this package by *airmail/ express*.	**Ik wil dit pakje per *luchtpost/expres* versturen.** ihk vihl diht pahk·yuh pehr *lukht·pohst/ehks·prehs* fuhr·stew·ruhn
Can I have a receipt?	**Mag ik een kwitantie?** mahkh ihk uhn kvee·tahnt·see

You May Hear...

Kunt u dit douaneaangifteformulier invullen? kuhnt ew dit doo·aa·nuh·aan·khihf·tuh·fohr·mew·leer ihn·fuh·luhn

Can you fill out the customs declaration form?

Hoeveel is dit waard? hoo·fayl ihs diht vaart

What's the value?

Wat zit hierin? vaht ziht heer·ihn

What's inside?

---

i **Postkantoren** (post offices) can be recognized by the **TNT POST** sign. Regular offices are open Monday–Friday from 9 a.m.–5 p.m. Some larger ones are open on Saturday mornings. Stamps can often be bought from tobacconists, news kiosks and stationery shops. Mailboxes are orange. The mailbox has two slots, one for letters in the local area (the mailbox indicates which post codes go into this slot) and one for all other letters. The latter is marked **overige bestemmingen** (other destinations).

▼ Food

Eating Out

Essential

Can you recommend a *good restaurant/bar*?	**Kunt u een *goed restaurant/goede bar* aanbevelen?** kuhnt ew uhn *khoot rehs·toa·rahnt/khoo·duh bahr* aan·buh·fay·luhn
Is there *a traditional Dutch/an inexpensive* restaurant near here?	**Is er een *traditioneel Nederlands/goedkoop* restaurant in de buurt?** ihs ehr uhn *traa·dee·shoa·nayl nay·duhr·lahnds/khoot·koap* rehs·toa·rahnt ihn duh bewrt
A table for…, please.	**Een tafel voor…, alstublieft.** uhn taa·fuhl foar…ahls·tew·bleeft
Can we sit…?	**Kunnen we…zitten?** kuh·nuhn vuh…zih·tuhn
– here/there	**– hier/daar** heer/daar
– outside	**– buiten** baw·tuhn
– in a non-smoking area	**– in het gedeelte voor niet-rokers** ihn heht khuh·dayl·tuh foar neet·roa·kuhrs
I'm waiting for someone.	**Ik wacht op iemand.** ihk vahkht ohp ee·mahnt
Where's the restroom [toilet]?	**Waar is het toilet?** vaar ihs heht tvaa·leht
Can I have a menu, please?	**Mag ik een menukaart, alstublieft?** mahkh ihk uhn muh·new·kaart ahls·tew·bleeft
What do you recommend?	**Wat kunt u aanbevelen?** vaht kuhnt ew aan·buh·fay·luhn
I'd like…	**Ik wil graag…** ihk vihl khraakh…
Some more…, please.	**Nog wat…, alstublieft.** nohkh vaht… ahls·tew·bleeft
Enjoy your meal.	**Eet smakelijk.** ayt smaa·kuh·luhk

Can I have the check [bill]?	**Mag ik de rekening?** mahkh ihk duh <u>ray</u>·kuh·nihng
Is service included?	**Is de bediening inbegrepen?** ihs duh buh·<u>dee</u>·nihng <u>ihn</u>·buh·<u>khray</u>·puhn
Can I pay by credit card?	**Kan ik met een creditcard betalen?** kahn ihk meht uhn <u>khreh</u>·diht·kaart buh·<u>taa</u>·luhn
Can I have a receipt, please?	**Mag ik een kwitantie, alstublieft?** mahkh ihk uhn kvee·<u>tahnt</u>·see ahls·tew·<u>bleeft</u>
Thank you.	**Dank u.** dahngk ew

Restaurant Types

Can you recommend...?	**Kunt u...aanbevelen?** kuhnt ew... <u>aan</u>·buh·<u>fay</u>·luhn
– a restaurant	**– een restaurant** uhn rehs·toa·<u>rahnt</u>
– a bar	**– een bar** uhn bahr
– a cafe	**– een café** uhn kaa·<u>fay</u>
– a fast-food place	**– een fastfoodrestaurant** uhn fahst·food·rehs·toa·<u>rahnt</u>

Reservations and Questions

I'd like to reserve a table...	**Ik wil graag een tafel reserveren...** ihk vihl khraakh uhn <u>taa</u>·fuhl ray·zuhr·<u>fay</u>·ruhn...
– for two	**– voor twee personen** foar tvay puhr·<u>soa</u>·nuhn
– for this evening	**– voor vanavond** foar fah·<u>naa</u>·fohnt
– for tomorrow at...	**– voor morgen om...** foar <u>mohr</u>·khuhn ohm...
A table for two, please.	**Een tafel voor twee personen, alstublieft.** uhn <u>taa</u>·fuhl foar tvay puhr·<u>soa</u>·nuhn ahls·tew·<u>bleeft</u>
We have a reservation.	**We hebben gereserveerd.** vuh <u>heh</u>·buhn khuh·<u>ray</u>·zuhr·<u>fayrt</u>
My name is...	**Mijn naam is...** mien naam ihs...
Where is the restroom [toilet]?	**Waar is het toilet?** vaar ihs heht tvaa·<u>leht</u>

You May Hear...

Heeft u gereserveerd? hayft ew khuh·<u>ray</u>·zuhr·<u>fayrt</u>	Do you have a reservation?
Voor hoeveel personen? foar <u>hoo</u>·fayl puhr·<u>soa</u>·nuhn	How many?
Roken of niet-roken? <u>roa</u>·kuhn ohf <u>neet</u>·<u>roa</u>·kuhn	Smoking or non-smoking?
Wilt u al bestellen? vihlt ew ahl buh·<u>steh</u>·luhn	Are you ready to order?
Wat mag het zijn? vaht mahkh heht zien	What would you like?
Ik kan...aanbevelen. ihk kahn... <u>aan</u>·buh·<u>fay</u>·luhn	I recommend...
Eet smakelijk. ayt <u>smaa</u>·kuh·luk	Enjoy your meal.

Ordering

Waiter/Waitress!	**Meneer/Mevrouw!** muh·<u>nayr</u>/muh·<u>frow</u>
We're ready to order.	**We willen graag bestellen.** vuh <u>vih</u>·luhn khraakh buh·<u>steh</u>·luhn
I'd like…	**Ik wil graag…** ihk vihl khraakh…
– a bottle of…	**– een fles…** uhn flehs…
– a carafe of…	**– een karaf…** uhn kah·<u>rahf</u>…
– a glass of…	**– een glas…** uhn khlahs…

▶ For alcoholic and non-alcoholic drinks, see page 71.

Can I have a menu?	**Mag ik de menukaart?** mahkh ihk duh muh·<u>new</u>·<u>kaart</u>
Do you have…?	**Heeft u…?** hayft ew…
– a menu in English	**– een menukaart in het Engels** uhn muh·<u>new</u>·<u>kaart</u> ihn heht <u>ehng</u>·uhls
– a fixed-price menu	**– een vast menu** uhn <u>fahst</u> muh·<u>new</u>
– a children's menu	**– een kindermenu** uhn <u>kihn</u>·duhr·muh·<u>new</u>
What do you recommend?	**Wat kunt u aanbevelen?** vaht kuhn ew <u>aan</u>·buh·<u>fay</u>·luhn
What's this?	**Wat is dit?** vaht ihs diht
What's in it?	**Wat zit erin?** vaht ziht ehr·<u>ihn</u>
It's to go [take away].	**Het is om mee te nemen.** heht ihs ohm <u>may</u> tuh <u>nay</u>·muhn

You May See...

COUVERT	cover charge
DAGSCHOTEL	menu of the day
BEDIENING (NIET) INBEGREPEN	service (not) included
SPECIALITEITEN	specials

Cooking Methods

baked	**gebakken** khuh·<u>bah</u>·kuhn
boiled	**gekookt** khuh·<u>koakt</u>
braised	**gesmoord** khuh·<u>smoart</u>
breaded	**gepaneerd** khuh·pah·<u>nayrt</u>
creamed	**met room bereid** meht roam buh·<u>riet</u>
diced	**in blokjes gesneden** ihn <u>blohk</u>·yuhs khuh·<u>snay</u>·duhn
fileted	**gefileerd** khuh·fee·<u>layrt</u>
fried	**gebakken** khuh·<u>bah</u>·kuhn
grilled	**gegrild** khuh·<u>khrihlt</u>
poached	**gepocheerd** khuh·poa·<u>shayrt</u>
roasted	**geroosterd** khuh·<u>roa</u>·stuhrt
sautéed	**gesauteerd** khuh·sow·<u>tayrt</u>
smoked	**gerookt** khuh·<u>roakt</u>
steamed	**gestoomd** khuh·<u>stoamt</u>
stewed	**gestoofd** khuh·<u>stoaft</u>
stuffed	**gevuld** khuh·<u>fuhlt</u>

Special Requirements

I'm *diabetic/ a vegetarian.*	**Ik ben *suikerpatiënt/vegetariër.*** ihk behn *<u>saw</u>·kuhr·paa·<u>shehnt</u>/<u>fay</u>·khuh·<u>taa</u>·ree·yuhr*
I'm lactose intolerant.	**Ik heb lactose-intolerantie.** ihk hehp <u>lahk</u>·<u>toa</u>·suh·ihn·<u>toh</u>·luh·<u>rahnt</u>·see
I'm allergic to...	**Ik ben allergisch voor...** ihk behn ah·<u>lehr</u>·gees foar...
I can't eat...	**Ik mag geen...eten.** ihk mahkh khayn... <u>ay</u>·tuhn
– dairy	**– zuivel** <u>zaw</u>·fuhl
– gluten	**– gluten** <u>khlew</u>·tuhn

– nuts	**– noten** <u>noa</u>·tuhn
– pork	**– varkensvlees** <u>fahr</u>·kuhns·flays
– shellfish	**– schelpdieren** <u>skhehlp</u>·dee·ruhn
– spicy food	**– pikante gerechten** <u>pee</u>·<u>kahn</u>·tuh khuh·<u>rehkh</u>·tuhn
– wheat	**– tarwe** <u>tahr</u>·vuh
Is it *halal/kosher*?	**Is het *halal/koosjer*?** ihs heht *haa·<u>lahl</u>/<u>koa</u>·shur*

Dining with Kids

Do you have children's portions?	**Heeft u kinderporties?** hayft ew <u>kihn</u>·duhr·pohr·<u>sees</u>
Can I have a highchair?	**Mag ik een kinderstoel?** mahkh ihk uhn <u>kihn</u>·duhr·stool
Where can I *feed/ change* the baby?	**Waar kan ik de baby *voeden/ verschonen*?** vaar kahn ihk duh <u>bay</u>·bee *<u>foo</u>·duhn/fuhr·<u>skhoa</u>·nuhn*
Can you warm this?	**Kunt u dit opwarmen?** kuhnt ew diht <u>ohp</u>·vahr·muhn

▶ For travel with children, see page 139.

Complaints

How much longer will our food be?	**Hoe lang moeten we nog op het eten wachten?** hoo lang <u>moo</u>·tuhn vuh nokh ohp heht <u>ay</u>·tuhn <u>vahkh</u>·tuhn
We can't wait any longer.	**We kunnen niet langer wachten.** vuh <u>kuh</u>·nuhn neet <u>lahng</u>·uhr vahkh·tuhn
We're leaving.	**We gaan weg.** vuh khaan vehkh
I didn't order this.	**Dat heb ik niet besteld.** daht hehp ihk neet buh·<u>stehlt</u>
I ordered…	**Ik heb om…gevraagd.** ihk hehp ohm… khuh·<u>fraakht</u>
I can't eat this.	**Dit kan ik niet eten.** diht kahn ihk neet <u>ay</u>·tuhn

This is too...	**Dit is te...** diht ihs tuh...
– cold/hot	**– koud/heet** kowt/hayt
– salty/spicy	**– zout/pikant** zowt/pee·<u>kahnt</u>
– tough/bland	**– taai/flauw** taay/flow
This isn't *clean/fresh*.	**Dit is niet *schoon/vers*.** diht ihs neet *skhoan/fehrs*

Paying

Can I have the check [bill]?	**Mag ik de rekening?** mahkh ihk duh <u>ray</u>·kuh·nihng
We'd like to pay separately.	**We willen graag apart betalen.** vuh <u>vih</u>·luhn khraakh aa·<u>pahrt</u> buh·<u>taa</u>·luhn
It's all together, please.	**Alles bij elkaar, alstublieft.** <u>ah</u>·luhs bie ehl·<u>kaar</u> ahls·tew·<u>bleeft</u>
Is service included?	**Is de bediening inbegrepen?** ihs duh buh·<u>dee</u>·nihng ihn·buh·<u>khray</u>·puhn
What's this amount for?	**Waar is dit bedrag voor?** vaar ihs diht buh·<u>drakh</u> foar
I didn't have that. I had...	**Dat heb ik niet gehad. Ik had...** daht hehp ihk neet khuh·<u>haht</u> ihk haht...
Can I pay by credit card?	**Kan ik met een creditcard betalen?** kahn ihk meht uhn <u>khreh</u>·diht·kaart buh·<u>taa</u>·luhn
Can I have an *itemized bill/a receipt*?	**Mag ik een *gespecificeerde rekening/ kwitantie*?** mahkh ihk uhn khuh·<u>spay</u>·see·fee·<u>sayr</u>·duh <u>ray</u>·kuh·nihng/ kvee·<u>tahnt</u>·see
That was a very good meal.	**Dat was een uitstekende maaltijd.** daht vahs uhn awt·<u>stay</u>·kuhn·duh <u>maal</u>·tiet

 Sales tax and service charges are already calculated into restaurant bills. Leaving as much as 10% is customary and appreciated, but not necessary.

Market

Where are the *carts [trolleys]*/*baskets*?	**Waar staan de *wagentjes/mandjes*?** vaar staan duh *vaa*·khun·*tyuhs*/*mahnt*·yuhs
Where *is/are*…?	**Waar *is/zijn*…?** vaar *ihs/zien*…

▶ For food items, see page 75.

I'd like some of *that/ those*.	**Ik wil graag wat van *dat/die*.** ihk vihl khraakh vaht fahn *daht/dee*
Can I taste it?	**Mag ik het proeven?** mahkh ihk heht <u>proo</u>·fuhn
I'd like…	**Ik wil graag…** ihk vihl khraakh…
– a *kilo/half-kilo* of…	**– een *kilo/pond*…** uhn <u>kee</u>·loa/pohnt…
– a *liter/half-liter* of…	**– een *liter/halve liter*…** uhn <u>lee</u>·tuhr/<u>hahl</u>·fuh <u>lee</u>·tuhr…
– a piece of…	**– een stukje…** uhn <u>stuhk</u>·yuh…
– a slice of…	**– een plakje…** uhn <u>plahk</u>·yuh…
More/Less than that.	**Meer/Minder dan dat.** mayr/<u>mihn</u>·duhr dahn daht
How much?	**Hoeveel kost het?** <u>hoo</u>·fayl kohst heht
Where do I pay?	**Waar moet ik betalen?** vaar moot ihk buh·<u>taa</u>·luhn
Can I have a bag?	**Mag ik een tas?** mahkh ihk uhn tahs
I'm being helped.	**Ik word al geholpen.** ihk vohrt ahl khuh·<u>hohl</u>·puhn

▶ For conversion tables, see page 163.

You May Hear…

Kan ik u helpen? kahn ihk ew <u>hehl</u>·puhn — Can I help you?
Wat mag het zijn? vaht mahkh heht zien — What would you like?
Anders nog iets? <u>ahn</u>·duhrs nokh eets — Anything else?
Het kost…euro. heht kohst…<u>u</u>·roa — That's…euros.

61

NA OPENEN HOUDBAAR TOT...	best if used by...
CALORIEËN	calories
VETVRIJ	fat free
GEKOELD BEWAREN	keep refrigerated
UITERSTE VERKOOPDATUM...	sell by...
GESCHIKT VOOR VEGETARIËRS	suitable for vegetarians

Dishes, Utensils and Kitchen Tools

bottle opener	**flesopener** flehs·oa·puh·nuhr
bowls	**kommen** koh·muhn
can opener	**blikopener** blihk·oa·puh·nuhr
corkscrew	**kurkentrekker** kuhr·kuhn·treh·kuhr
cups	**kopjes** kohp·yuhs
forks	**vorken** fohr·kuhn
frying pan	**koekenpan** koo·kuhn·pahn
glasses	**glazen** khlaa·zuhn
knives	**messen** meh·suhn
measuring *cup/ spoon*	**maatbeker/maatlepel** maat·bay·kuhr/maat·lay·puhl
napkins	**servetten** sehr·feh·tuhn
plates	**borden** bohr·duhn
pot	**pot** poht
saucepan	**steelpan** stayl·pahn
spatula	**spatel** spaa·tuhl
spoons	**lepels** lay·puhls

Meals

i **Ontbijt** (breakfast) is usually eaten between 7 and 10 a.m. (if eaten at all) and consists of coffee and toast with jam or **hagelslag** (chocolate sprinkles). **Lunch** (lunch) is served from 12–2 p.m. It is usually a light meal involving bread or rolls with cheese and cold cuts. **Avondeten** (dinner), from 6–8 p.m., is the main meal of the day and may include soup, potatoes, meat and vegetables followed by dessert.

Breakfast

boter <u>boa</u>·tuhr	butter
brood broat	bread
broodje <u>broat</u>·yuh	roll
ei <u>ie</u>	egg
roerei <u>roor</u>·le	scrambled egg
honing <u>hoa</u>·nihng	honey
jam zhehm	jam
koffie *met/zonder* melk <u>koh</u>·fee meht/<u>zohn</u>·duhr mehlk	coffee *with/without* milk
melk mehlk	milk
thee tay	tea
roggebrood <u>roh</u>·khuh·broat	rye bread
toast toast	toast
vruchtensap <u>fruhkh</u>·tuhn·sahp	fruit juice

I'd like…	**Ik wil graag…** ihk vihl khraakh…
More…please.	**Ik wil graag nog wat…, alctublieft.** ihk vihl khraakh nohkh vaht…ahls·tew·<u>bleeft</u>

Appetizers [Starters]

gerookte paling	khuh·<u>roak</u>·tuh <u>paa</u>·lihng	smoked eel
huzarensalade	hew·<u>zaa</u>·ruhn·saa·<u>laa</u>·duh	potato, vegetables and meat with mayonnaise
mosselen	<u>moh</u>·suh·luhn	mussels
nieuwe haring	<u>neeew</u>·vuh <u>haa</u>·rihng	freshly caught, salt-cured herring
oester	<u>oos</u>·tuhr	oyster
pasteitje	pahs·<u>tie</u>·tyuh	pastry filled with meat or fish
Russisch ei	<u>ruh</u>·see·suh <u>ie</u>	hard-boiled egg filled with mayonnaise
zure haring	<u>zew</u>·ruh <u>haa</u>·ring	pickled herring

Soup

aardappelsoep	<u>aar</u>·dah·puhl·soep	potato soup
aspergesoep	ahs·<u>pehr</u>·zhuh·soep	asparagus soup
bouillon	boo·<u>yohn</u>	broth
bruinebonensoep	<u>braw</u>·nuh <u>boa</u>·nuhn soep	bean soup
erwtensoep	<u>ehr</u>·tuhn·soep	famous thick Dutch pea soup with pig's knuckle, smoked sausage and bacon
gebonden soep	khuh·<u>bohn</u>·duhn soep	cream soup
groentesoep (met balletjes) <u>khroon</u>·tuh·soep (meht <u>bah</u>·luh·tyuhs)		vegetable soup (with meatballs)
heldere soep	<u>hehl</u>·duh·ruh soep	consommé

With/Without…	**Met/Zonder…** meht/<u>zohn</u>·duhr…	
I can't have…	**Ik mag geen…eten.** ihk mahkh khayn…<u>ay</u>·tuhn	

kippensoep <u>kih</u>·puhn·soop	chicken soup
koninginnensoep <u>koa</u>·nihng·<u>ih</u>·nuhn·soop	cream of chicken soup
ossenstaartsoep <u>oh</u>·suhn·staart·soop	oxtail soup
tomatensoep toa·<u>maa</u>·tuhn·soop	tomato soup
uiensoep <u>aw</u>·yuhn·soop	onion soup
vermicellisoep <u>vehr</u>·mee·<u>seh</u>·lee·soop	clear noodle soup
vissoep <u>fihs</u>·soop	fish soup

The Netherlands has a mild climate, though it is often cool and rains a lot, which may explain the heaviness of the food. A very famous traditional winter dish is **erwtensoep** (pea soup), made from peas, winter vegetables and chunks of sausage or ham. It is typically served with crusty bread. In a good **erwtensoep** you should be able to stand your spoon upright.

Fish and Seafood

forel <u>foa</u>·rehl	trout
garnaal khahr·<u>naal</u>	shrimp [prawn]
gerookte paling khuh·<u>roak</u>·tuh <u>paa</u>·lihng	smoked eel
haring <u>haa</u>·rihng	herring [whitebait]
haringsalade <u>haa</u>·rihng·saa·<u>laa</u>·duh	salad of herring, potatoes, beets, apples, pickles and mayonnaise
inktvis <u>ihnkt</u>·fihs	squid
kabeljauw <u>kaa</u>·buhl·<u>yow</u>	cod

I'd like…	**Ik wil graag…** ihk vihl khraakh…
More…please.	**Ik wil graag nog wat…, alstublieft.** ihk vihl khraakh nohkh vaht…ahls·tew·<u>bleeft</u>

krab krahp	crab
kreeft krayft	lobster
makreel maa·<u>krayl</u>	mackerel
mossel <u>moh</u>·suhl	mussel
nieuwe haring <u>neeew</u>·vuh <u>haa</u>·rihng	freshly caught, salt-cured herring
octopus <u>ohk</u>·toa·puhs	octopus
oester <u>oos</u>·tuhr	oyster
paling <u>paa</u>·lihng	eel
sardientje sahr·<u>deen</u>·tyuh	sardine
schelvis <u>skhehl</u>·fihs	haddock
schol skhol	plaice
stokvisschotel <u>stohk</u>·fihs·<u>skhoa</u>·tuhl	stew of dried cod, potatoes, rice, onions
tong tohng	sole
tonijn toa·<u>nien</u>	tuna
schelpdier <u>skehlp</u>·deer	clam
zalm zahlm	salmon

Meat and Poultry

biefstuk <u>beef</u>·stuhk	steak
blinde vink <u>blihn</u>·duh <u>fihnk</u>	stuffed slices of veal
duif dawf	pigeon
eend aynt	duck
fazant faa·<u>sahnt</u>	pheasant
gans khahns	goose

With/Without…	**Met/Zonder…** meht/<u>zohn</u>·duhr…
I can't have…	**Ik mag geen…eten.** ihk mahkh khayn…<u>ay</u>·tuhn

haas haas	hare
jachtschotel <u>yahkht</u>·skhoa·tuhl	meat casserole with potatoes
kalfsvlees <u>kahlfs</u>·flays	veal
kalkoen kahl·<u>koon</u>	turkey
kip kihp	chicken
konijn koa·<u>nien</u>	rabbit
lamsvlees <u>lahms</u>·flays	lamb
parelhoen <u>paa</u>·ruhl·hoon	guinea fowl
piepkuiken peep·<u>kaw</u>·kuhn	spring chicken
rundvlees <u>ruhnt</u>·flays	beef
spek spehk	bacon
varkensvlees <u>fahr</u>·kuhns·flays	pork
wienerschnitzel <u>vee</u>·nuhr <u>shniht</u>·suhl	breaded veal chops
worst <u>vohrst</u>	sausage

rare	**kort gebakken** kohrt khuh·<u>bah</u>·kuhn	
medium	**medium** <u>may</u>·dee·yuhm	
well-done	**goed doorbakken** khoot doar·<u>bah</u>·kuhn	

Vegetables

aardappel <u>aar</u>·dah·puhl	potato
andijvie ahn·<u>die</u>·vee	endives
bietje <u>beet</u>·yuh	beetroot
bloemkool <u>bloom</u>·koal	cauliflower

I'd like…	**Ik wil graag…** ihk vihl khraakh…
More…please.	**Ik wil graag nog wat…, alstublieft.** ihk vihl khraakh nohkh vaht…ahls·tew·<u>bleeft</u>

champignon shahm·<u>pee</u>·yohn	mushroom
erwt <u>ehrt</u>	pea
knoflook <u>knohf</u>·loak	garlic
komkommer kohm·<u>kohm</u>·muhr	cucumber
kool koal	cabbage
paprika (rode/groene) <u>paa</u>·pree·kaa (<u>roa</u>·duh/<u>khroo</u>·nuh)	(red/green) pepper
raap raap	turnip
rabarber <u>raa</u>·bahr·buhr	rhubarb
selderij <u>sehl</u>·duh·rie	celery
sla slaa	lettuce
sperziebonen spehr·see·<u>boa</u>·nuhn	green beans
stamppot van boerenkool met rookworst <u>stahm</u>·poht fahn <u>boo</u>·ruhn·koal meht <u>roak</u>·vohrst	kale and potatoes, with smoked sausage
ui aw	onion

With/Without…	**Met/Zonder…** meht/<u>zohn</u>·duhr…
I can't have…	**Ik mag geen…eten.** ihk mahkh khayn…<u>ay</u>·tuhn

witlof <u>viht</u>·lohf	Belgian endive
witte asperge (met saus) <u>vih</u>·tuh <u>ah</u>·spehr·zhuh (meht sows)	white asparagus (with sauce)
wortel <u>vohr</u>·tuhl	carrot
zuurkool <u>zewr</u>·koal	sauerkraut

Spices and Staples

aardappel <u>aar</u>·dah·puhl	potato
kruiden <u>kraw</u>·duhn	herbs
pasta <u>pahs</u>·taa	pasta
peper <u>pay</u>·puhr	pepper (seasoning)
rijst riest	rice
zout zowt	salt

Fruit

aardbei <u>aart</u>·bie	strawberry
ananas <u>ah</u>·naa·nahs	pineapple
appel <u>ah</u>·puhl	apple
banaan baa·<u>naan</u>	banana
braam braam	blackberry
druif drawf	grape
framboos frahm·<u>boas</u>	raspberry
granaatappel khraa·<u>naat</u>·ah·puhl	pomegranate
grapefruit <u>grayp</u>·froot	grapefruit
kers kehrs	cherry
mandarijn <u>mahn</u>·daa·<u>rien</u>	tangerine

I'd like…	**Ik wil graag…** ihk vihl khraakh …
More…please.	**Ik wil graag nog wat…, alstublieft.** ihk vihl khraakh nohkh vaht…ahls·tew·<u>bleeft</u>

mango <u>mahn</u>·goa	mango
meloen muh·<u>loon</u>	melon
nectarine nehk·taa·<u>ree</u>·nuh	nectarine
perzik <u>pehr</u>·zihk	peach
pruim prawm	plum
rode bes <u>roa</u>·duh <u>behs</u>	red currant
sinaasappel <u>see</u>·naas·ah·puhl	orange
watermeloen <u>vaa</u>·tuhr·muh·loon	watermelon

Cheese

Edammer kaas <u>ay</u>·dah·muhr kaas	Edam mild cheese
Friese nagelkaas <u>free</u>·suh <u>naa</u>·khuhl·kaas	cheese from Friesland, made with skimmed milk and cloves
geitenkaas <u>khie</u>·tuhn·kaas	goat's cheese
Goudse kaas <u>khowt</u>·suh kaas	famous Gouda cheese
komijnekaas koa·<u>mie</u>·nuh·kaas	mild, hard cheese with cumin seeds; also called **Leidse kaas**
Leerdammer kaas <u>layr</u>·dah·muhr kaas	sweet, nutty cheese
Maaslander kaas <u>maas</u>·lahn·duhr kaas	Gouda-like cheese

Dessert

appeltaart <u>ah</u>·puhl·taart	Dutch apple tart
chipolatapudding <u>shee</u>·poa·<u>laa</u>·taa·<u>puh</u>·dihng	pudding of eggs, biscuits and liqueur

With/Without…	**Met/Zonder…** meht/<u>zohn</u>·duhr…
I can't have…	**Ik mag geen…eten.** ihk mahkh khayn…<u>ay</u>·tuhn

gebak khuh·<u>bahk</u>	pastry or cake
Haagse bluf <u>haakh</u>·suh bluhf	whipped egg whites with currant sauce
kwarktaart <u>kvahrk</u>·taart	light cheesecake
pannenkoek <u>pah</u>·nuhn·<u>kook</u>	thin pancake
poffertje <u>poh</u>·fuhr·tyuh	tiny sugared pancake
vla flaa	custard
vruchtenvlaai <u>fruhkh</u>·tuhn·flaay	Limburg fruit flan
wafel <u>vaa</u>·fuhl	waffle

i In the Netherlands, you'll find many **pannenkoekhuisjes** (pancake restaurants), which offer entire menus of sweet and savory pancakes. A traditional combination is **spekpannenkoek met stroop** (with bacon and syrup), substantial enough for a whole meal! Though **pannenkoeken** tend to be thick, there is a very popular thin variety called **flensjes**.

Drinks

Essential

May I see the *wine list/drink menu*?	**Mag ik de *wijnkaart/drankkaart* zien?** mahkh ihk duh <u>*vien*</u>·*kaart/<u>drahnk</u>·kaart* zeen
What do you recommend?	**Wat kunt u aanbevelen?** vaht kuhnt ew <u>aan</u>·buh·fay·luhn
I'd like a *bottle/glass* of *red/white* wine.	**Ik wil graag een *fles/glas rode/witte* wijn.** ihk vihl khraakh uhn *flehs/khlahs <u>roa</u>·duh/<u>vih</u>·tuh* vien
May I have the house wine?	**Mag ik de huiswijn?** mahkh ihk duh <u>haws</u>·vien

Another *bottle/glass*, please.	**Nog een *fles/glas*, alstublieft.** nohkh uhn *flehs/khlahs* ahls·tew·<u>bleeft</u>
I'd like a local beer.	**Ik wil graag een lokaal biertje.** ihk yihl khraakh uhn loa·<u>kaal</u> <u>beer</u>·tyuh
Can I buy you a drink?	**Wilt u iets van me drinken?** vihlt ew eets fahn muh <u>drihng</u>·kuhn
Cheers!	**Proost!** proast
A *coffee/tea*, please.	**Een *koffie/thee*, alstublieft.** uhn <u>koh</u>·fee/tay ahls·tew·<u>bleeft</u>
With/Without milk.	***Met/Zonder* melk.** meht/<u>zohn</u>·duhr mehlk
With sugar.	**Met suiker.** meht <u>zaw</u>·kuhr
With artificial sweetener.	**Met zoetjes.** meht <u>zoo</u>·tyuhs
..., please.	**..., alstublieft.** ...ahls·tew·<u>bleeft</u>
– Juice	**– Een vruchtensap** uhn <u>fruhkh</u>·tuhn·sahp
– Soda	**– Een frisdrank** uhn <u>frihs</u>·drahngk
– (*Sparkling/Still*) Water	**– (*Koolzuurhoudend/Koolzuurvrij*) Water** (<u>koal</u>·zewr·<u>how</u>·duhnt/<u>koal</u>·zewr·<u>frie</u>) <u>vaa</u>·tuhr

Non-alcoholic Drinks

appelsap <u>ah</u>·puhl·sahp	apple juice
cola <u>koa</u>·laa	cola
chocomel shoa·koa·<u>mehl</u>	chocolate milk
frisdrank <u>frihs</u>·drahngk	soda
grapefruitsap <u>grayp</u>·froot	grapefruit juice
koffie <u>koh</u>·fee	coffee
limonade <u>lee</u>·moa·naa·duh	lemonade
mineraalwater <u>mee</u>·nuh·<u>raal</u>·vaa·tuhr	mineral water

sinaasappelsap <u>see</u>·naas·ah·puhl	orange juice
thee tay	tea
warme chocolademelk <u>vahr</u>·muh shoa·koa·<u>laa</u>·duh·mehlk	hot chocolate

Een kopje koffie met gebak (a mid-morning coffee, accompanied by a pastry), is somewhat of a Dutch ritual. Coffee is usually brewed strong and may be drunk black, with a little **koffiemelk** (condensed milk) or **slagroom** (whipped cream).

Tea is brewed weak and is usually drunk without milk, sometimes **met citroen** (with lemon). **Kruidenthee** (herb tea), such as mint tea, and English tea are also popular.

You May Hear...

Mag ik u een drankje aanbieden? mahkh ihk ew uhn <u>drangk</u>·yuh <u>aan</u>·bee·duhn	Can I get you a drink?
Met *melk/suiker*? meht mehlk/<u>zaw</u>·kuhr	With *milk/sugar*?
***Koolzuurhoudend/Koolzuurvrij* water?** <u>koal</u>·zewr·<u>how</u>·duhnt/<u>koal</u>·zewr·<u>frie</u> <u>vaa</u>·tuhr	*Sparkling/Still* water?

Aperitifs, Cocktails and Liqueurs

advocaat aht·foa·<u>kaat</u>
famous Dutch egg liqueur

brandewijn <u>brahn</u>·duh·vien
Dutch brandy

cognac kohn·<u>yahk</u>
brandy

gin-tonic zhihn·<u>toh</u>·nihk
gin and tonic

jenever yuh·<u>nay</u>·vuhr
Dutch gin

oranjebitter oa·<u>rahn</u>·yuh·bih·tuhr
slightly bitter liqueur

whisky <u>vihs</u>·kee
whisky

wodka <u>vohd</u>·kaa
vodka

Beer

bier/pils beer/pihls
beer/lager

donker bier <u>dohng</u>·kuhr beer
dark beer

flessenbier <u>fleh</u>·suhn·beer
bottled beer

getapt bier khuh·<u>tahpt</u> beer
draft [draught] beer

licht bier likht beer
light beer

oud bruin owt brawn
"old brown": a dark, slightly sweet stout

> *i*
> The Dutch are internationally famous for **pilsener** or **pils** (lager) beer. Brands like Amstel™, Heineken™ and Grolsch™ are sold around the world. In the Netherlands, beer might even be drunk as **aperitief** (an aperitif) or instead of a **borrel** (usually **jenever**, the Dutch equivalent of gin). In fact, a good beer is often more deeply appreciated than a good wine.

Wine

droge <u>droa</u>·khuh
dry

huiswijn <u>haws</u>·vien
house wine

mousserende moo·<u>say</u>·run·duh	sparkling
rode <u>roa</u>·duh	red
rosé <u>roa</u>·say	blush [rosé]
wijn vien	wine
witte <u>vih</u>·tuh	white
zoete <u>zoo</u>·tuh	sweet

Menu Reader

aalbes <u>aal</u>·behs	red currant
aardappel <u>aar</u>·dah·puhl	potato
aardappelpuree <u>aar</u>·dah·puhl·pew·<u>ray</u>	mashed potato
aardappelsalade <u>aar</u>·dah·puhl·saa·<u>laa</u>·duh	potato salad
aardappelsoep <u>aar</u>·dah·puhl·<u>soop</u>	potato soup
aardbei <u>aart</u>·bie	strawberry

abrikoos aa·bree·<u>koas</u>	apricot
advocaat aht·foa·<u>kaat</u>	egg liqueur
amandel ah·<u>mahn</u>·duhl	almond
amandelgebak ah·<u>mahn</u>·duhl·khuh·<u>bahk</u>	almond tart
Amsterdamse ui ahm·stuhr·<u>dahm</u>·suh aw	pickled onion
ananas <u>ah</u>·naa·nahs	pineapple
andijvie ahn·<u>die</u>·vee	endive
andijviesla ahn·<u>die</u>·vee·<u>slaa</u>	endive salad
anijs aa·<u>nies</u>	aniseed
anijslikeur aa·<u>nies</u>·lee·<u>kur</u>	aniseed liqueur
anijsmelk aa·<u>nies</u>·mehlk	aniseed milk
ansjovis ahn·<u>shoa</u>·fihs	anchovies
aperitief aa·puh·ree·<u>teef</u>	aperitif
appel <u>ah</u>·puhl	apple
appelbol <u>ah</u>·puhl·bohl	apple dumpling
appelflap <u>ah</u>·puhl·flahp	apple turnover
appelmoes <u>ah</u>·puhl·moos	apple sauce
appeltaart <u>ah</u>·puhl·taart	apple pie or tart
artisjok ahr·tee·<u>shohk</u>	artichoke
asperge ahs·<u>pehr</u>·zhuh	asparagus
aspergesoep ahs·<u>pehr</u>·zhuh·soop	asparagus soup
aubergine oa·behr·<u>zhee</u>·nuh	eggplant [aubergine]
augurk ow·<u>khuhr</u>k	gherkin
avocado aa·voa·<u>kaa</u>·doa	avocado
baars baars	bass, perch
babyinktvis <u>bay</u>·bee·<u>ihngkt</u>·fihs	baby squid
babyoctopus <u>bay</u>·bee·ohk·toa·puhs	baby octopus
baguette <u>baa</u>·geht	French bread

bami baa·mee	Chinese or Indonesian noodles
bami goreng baa·mee khoa·rehng	fried Chinese or Indonesian noodles
banaan baa·naan	banana
banketletter bahn·keht·leh·tuhr	pastry in letter shape with almond filling
basilicum baa·see·lee·kuhm	basil
bataat baa·taat	sweet potato
bavarois baa·vaar·vah	Bavarian cream
beignet behn·yay	fritter
beschuit buh·skawt	Dutch toast
bes behs	berry
biefstuk beef·stuhk	pan-fried steak
biefstuk van de haas beef·stuhk fahn duh haas	porterhouse steak
bier beer	beer
bieslook bees·loak	chives
bietje beet·yuh	beet [beetroot]
biscuit bihs·kvee	biscuit
bitterbal bih·tuhr·bahl	breaded meatball
bladerdeeg blaa·duhr·daykh	puff pastry
blauwe druif blow·uh drawf	red grape
bleekselderij blayk·sehl·duh·rie	celery
blikgroente blihk·khroon·tuh	canned vegetable
blinde vink blihn·duh fihnk	beef or veal meat roll
bloedworst bloot·wohrst	black pudding
bloem bloom	flour
bloemkool bloom·koal	cauliflower
boerenjongens boo·ruhn·yohng·uhns	brandy with raisins

boerenkool <u>boo</u>·ruhn·koal	kale
boerenmeisjes <u>boo</u>·ruhn·<u>mies</u>·yuhs	brandy with apricots
boerenomelet <u>boo</u>·ruhn·oh·muh·<u>leht</u>	omelet with potatoes, vegetables and bacon
bonen <u>boa</u>·nuhn	beans
borrel <u>boh</u>·ruhl	aperitif
borreltje <u>boh</u>·ruhl·tyuh	alcoholic drink
borst bohrst	breast
bosbes <u>bohs</u>·behs	blueberry
boter <u>boa</u>·tuhr	butter
boterbabbelaar <u>boa</u>·tuhr·bah·buh·laar	butterscotch
boterboon <u>boa</u>·tuhr·boan	butter bean
boterkoek <u>boa</u>·tuhr·kook	butter cookie [biscuit]
bouillon boo·<u>yohn</u>	broth
bourbon <u>bur</u>·buhn	bourbon
bout bowt	leg (cut of meat)
bowl boal	punch
braadstuk <u>braat</u>·stuhk	roast
braam braam	blackberry
brandewijn <u>brahn</u>·duh·vien	brandy
brasem <u>braa</u>·suhm	bream
brood broat	bread
broodje <u>broat</u>·yuh	bun, roll
broodkruimels <u>broat</u>·kraw·muhls	breadcrumbs
bruine boon <u>braw</u>·nuh boan	brown bean
bruinebonensoep braw·nuh·<u>boa</u>·nuhn·soop	brown bean soup
caffeïnevrij kaa·fay·<u>ee</u>·nuh·frie	decaffeinated
cake kayk	cake, sponge cake

caramelpudding kaa·raa·<u>mehl</u>·puh·dihng — caramel pudding

champignon shahm·pee·<u>yohn</u> — mushroom

cantharel kahn·tah·<u>rehl</u> — chanterelle mushroom

cantharellensoep kahn·tah·<u>reh</u>·luhn·soop — chanterelle mushroom soup

chipolatapudding shee·poa·<u>laa</u>·taa·puh·dihng — pudding of eggs, cookies [biscuits] and liqueur

chocolade shoa·koa·<u>laa</u>·duh — chocolate

chocomel shoa·koa·<u>mehl</u> — chocolate milk

citroen see·<u>troon</u> — lemon

citroengras see·<u>troon</u>·khrahs — lemongrass

citroensap see·<u>troon</u>·sahp — lemon juice

cognac kohn·<u>yahk</u> — brandy

consommé kohn·soh·<u>may</u> — consommé

cornflakes kohrn·flayks — cereal

courgette koor·<u>zheht</u> — zucchini [courgette]

dadels <u>daa</u>·duhls — dates

dagschotel <u>dahkh</u>·skhoa·tuhl — dish of the day

dessert/toetje deh·<u>sehrt</u>/<u>toot</u>·yuh — dessert

dessertwijn deh·<u>sehrt</u>·vien — dessert wine

dille <u>dih</u>·luh — dill

diner/avondeten dee·<u>nay</u>/<u>aa</u>·fohnt·<u>ay</u>·tuhn — dinner

donut <u>doa</u>·nuht — doughnut

dooier <u>doa</u>·yuhr — egg yolk

doperwt <u>dohp</u>·ehrt — garden pea

dragon <u>draa</u>·khohn — tarragon

drilpudding <u>drihl</u>·puh·dihng — jelly

druif drawf	grape
duif dawf	pigeon
Edammer kaas ay·dah·muhr kaas	Edam cheese
eekhoorntjesbrood ayk·hoarn·tyuhs·broat	porcini mushroom
eend aynt	duck
eidooier ie·doa·yuhr	egg yolk
eieren ie·yuh·ruhn	eggs
eiergerecht ie·yuhr·khuh·rehkht	egg dish
eigengemaakt ie·khuhn·khuh·maakt	homemade
eiwit ie·wiht	egg white
entrecote ahn·truh·coat	sirloin steak
erwt ehrt	pea
erwtensoep ehr·tuhn·soop	pea soup
fazant faa·zahnt	pheasant
filet fee·lay	fillet
flensje flehns·yuh	thin, small pancake
flessenbier fleh·suhn·beer	bottled beer
foelie foo·lee	mace (spice)
forel foa·rehl	trout
framboos frahm·boas	raspberry
fricandeau free·kahn·doa	meat with sauce
Friese nagelkaas free·suh naa·khuhl·kaas	cheese with cloves
frisdrank frihs·drahngk	soda
gadogado khaa·doa·khaa·doa	Indonesian mixture of vegetables, cucumber and tofu
gans khahns	goose
garnaal khahr·naal	shrimp [prawn]

80

garnering khar·<u>nay</u>·rihng	garnish, trimming
gebak khuh·<u>bahk</u>	pastry
gebakken kip khuh·<u>bah</u>·kuhn kihp	fried chicken
gebonden soep khuh·<u>bohn</u>·duhn	cream soup
gedroogde dadels khuh·<u>droakh</u>·duh <u>daa</u>·duhls	dried dates
gedroogde pruimen khuh·<u>droakh</u>·duh <u>praw</u>·muhn	dried prunes
gedroogde vijgen khuh·<u>droakh</u>·duh <u>fie</u>khuhn	dried figs
gegrilde kip khuh·<u>khrihl</u>·duh kihp	grilled chicken
gehakt khuh·<u>hahkt</u>	ground meat [mincemeat]
gehaktbal khuh·<u>hahkt</u>·bahl	meatball
geit khiet	goat
geltenkaas <u>khie</u>·tuhn·kaas	goat cheese
gekonfijte vrucht khuh·kohn·<u>fie</u>·tuh fruhkht	candied fruit
gekookt eitje khuh·<u>koakt</u> <u>ie</u>·tyuh	boiled egg
gekookte aardappel khuh·<u>koak</u>·tuh <u>aar</u>·dah·puhl	boiled potato
gele spercieboon <u>khay</u>·luh <u>spehr</u>·see·boan	butter bean
gember <u>khehm</u>·buhr	ginger
gemengde grill khuh·<u>mehng</u>·duh khrihl	mixed grill
gemengde groenten khuh·<u>mehng</u>·duh <u>khroon</u>·tuhn	mixed vegetables
gemengde kruiden khuh·<u>mehng</u>·duh <u>kraw</u>·duhn	mixed herbs
gemengde noten khuh·<u>mehng</u>·duh <u>noa</u>·tuhn	assorted nuts
gemengde salade khuh·<u>mehng</u>·duh saa·<u>laa</u>·duh	mixed salad
gerookte paling khuh·<u>roak</u>·tuh <u>paa</u>·lihng	smoked eel

gerookte zalm khuh·<u>roak</u>·tuh zahlm	smoked salmon
geroosterd brood khuh·<u>roas</u>·tuhrt broat	toast
geroosterde aardappel khuh·<u>roas</u>·tuhr·duh <u>aar</u>·dah·puhl	roast potato
geroosterde kip khuh·<u>roas</u>·tuhr·duh kihp	roast chicken
gestoofd fruit khuh·<u>stoaft</u> frawt	stewed fruit
gestoomde vis khuh·<u>stoam</u>·duh fihs	steamed fish
getapt bier khuh·<u>tahpt</u> beer	draft [draught] beer
gevogelte khuh·<u>foa</u>·khuhl·tuh	fowl
gevulde olijf khuh·<u>fuhl</u>·duh oa·<u>lief</u>	stuffed olive
gezouten pinda khuh·<u>zow</u>·tuhn <u>pihn</u>·dah	salted peanut
gin-tonic zhihn·<u>toh</u>·nihk	gin and tonic
goulash <u>khoo</u>·lahsh	goulash
grapefruit <u>krayp</u>·froot	grapefruit
granaatappel khraa·<u>naat</u>·ah·puhl	pomegranate
griesmeelpudding <u>khrees</u>·mayl·puh·dihng	semolina pudding
groene erwt <u>khroo</u>·nuh ehrt	green pea
groene paprika <u>khroo</u>·nuh <u>paa</u>·pree·kaa	green pepper
groene salade <u>khroo</u>·nuh saa·<u>laa</u>·duh	green salad
groentebouillon <u>khroon</u>·tuh·boo·<u>yohn</u>	vegetable broth
groente <u>khroon</u>·tuh	vegetable
groentesoep <u>khroon</u>·tuh·soop	vegetable soup
Goudse kaas <u>khowt</u>·suh kaas	Gouda cheese
guave <u>kwaa</u>·fuh	guava
Haagse bluf <u>haakh</u>·suh bluhf	dessert of whipped egg white with red currant sauce
haas haas	hare
hachee <u>hah</u>·shay	meat stew

hamlap <u>hahm</u>·lahp	pork steak
hapje <u>hahp</u>·yuh	snack
hapjes vooraf <u>hahp</u>·yuhs foar·<u>ahf</u>	appetizers
hardgekookt hahrt·khuh·<u>koakt</u>	hard-boiled (egg)
harder <u>hahr</u>·duhr	gray mullet
haring <u>haa</u>·rihng	herring
haringsalade <u>haa</u>·rihng·saa·laa·duh	salad of salted or marinated herring
havermoutpap <u>haa</u>·fuhr·mowt·pahp	porridge
hazelnoten <u>haa</u>·zuhl·noa·tuhn	hazelnuts
heek hayk	hake
heet water hayt <u>vaa</u>·tuhr	hot water
heilbot <u>hiel</u>·boht	halibut
heldere soep <u>hehl</u>·duh·ruh soop	broth
hete bliksem <u>hay</u>·tuh <u>blihk</u>·suhm	dish of potatoes, bacon and apple
hete pepersaus <u>hay</u>·tuh <u>pay</u>·purh·sows	hot pepper sauce
Hollandse biefstuk <u>hoh</u>·lahnt·suh <u>beef</u>·stuhk	Dutch steak
honing <u>hoa</u>·nihng	honey
hoorntje <u>hoarn</u>·tyuh	cream horn (dessert)
hopjes <u>hohp</u>·yuhs	coffee-flavored toffee
huiswijn <u>haws</u>·vien	house wine
hutspot <u>huhts</u>·poht	stew made of mashed potatoes with carrots and onions or with curly kale
hutspot met klapstuk <u>huhts</u>·poht meht <u>klahp</u>·stuhk	mashed potatoes, carrots and onions served with rib of beef

huzarensalade hew·<u>zaa</u>·ruhn·saa·laa·duh — mixture of potato, raw vegetables and meat with mayonnaise

ijs ies — ice

in beslag gebakken ihn buh·<u>slahkh</u> khuh·<u>bah</u>·kuhn — fried in batter

in de pan gebakken vis ihn duh pahn khuh·<u>bah</u>·kuhn fihs — fried fish

in knoflook ihn <u>knohf</u>·loak — in garlic

in olie ihn <u>oa</u>·lee — in oil

in de oven gebakken vis ihn duh <u>oa</u>·fuhn khuh·<u>bah</u>·kuhn fihs — baked fish

inktvis <u>ihnkt</u>·fihs — squid

inwendige organen ihn·<u>wehn</u>·dih·khuh ohr·<u>khaa</u>·nuhn — giblets

jachtschotel <u>yahkht</u>·skhoa·tuhl — meat casserole with potatoes

jam zhehm — jam

jenever yuh·<u>nay</u>·vuhr — gin

jeneverbes yuh·<u>nay</u>·vuhr·behs — juniper berry

jong geitenvlees yohng <u>khie</u>·tuhn·flays — young goat

jonge eend <u>yohng</u>·uh aynt — duckling

jus zhew — gravy

kaas kaas — cheese

kaasplank <u>kaas</u>·plahnk — cheese board

kabeljauw <u>kaa</u>·buhl·yow — cod

kalfskarbonade <u>kahlfs</u>·kahr·boa·<u>naa</u>·duh — veal chop

kalfsoester <u>kahlfs</u>·oos·tuhr — veal escalope

kalfsvlees <u>kahlfs</u>·flays — veal

kalfszwezerik <u>kahlfs</u>·zvay·zuh·rihk — sweetbread

kalkoen kahl·<u>koon</u>	turkey
kammossel <u>kahm</u>·moh·suhl	scallop
kaneel kaa·<u>nayl</u>	cinnamon
kappertje <u>kah</u>·puhr·tyuh	caper
karbonade karh·boa·<u>naa</u>·duh	chop
karnemelk <u>kahr</u>·nuh·mehlk	buttermilk
karwij kahr·<u>wie</u>	caraway
kastanje kahs·<u>tahn</u>·yus	chestnut
katenspek <u>kaa</u>·tuhn·spehk	smoked bacon
kaviaar kaa·vee·<u>yaar</u>	caviar
kers <u>kehrs</u>	cherry
kerstomaat <u>kehrs</u>·toa·maat	cherry tomato
kervel <u>kehr</u>·fuhl	chervil
kidneyboon <u>kiht</u>·nee·boan	kidney bean
kikkererwt <u>kih</u>·kuhr·ehrt	chickpea
kip klhp	chicken
kippenborst <u>kih</u>·puhn·bohrst	breast of chicken
kippenlever <u>kih</u>·puhn·lay·fuhr	chicken liver
kippensoep <u>kih</u>·puhn·soop	chicken soup
kiwi <u>kee</u>·vee	kiwi
klapstuk <u>klahp</u>·stuhk	beef rib
kluif klawf	pig's knuckle
knakworst <u>knahk</u>·vohrst	wiener
knoedel <u>knoo</u>·duhl	dumpling
knoflook <u>knohf</u>·loak	garlic
knoflookmayonaise <u>knohf</u>·loak·maa·yoh·neh·suh	garlic mayonnaise

knoflooksaus <u>knohf</u>·loak·sows	garlic sauce
knolselderij <u>knohl</u>·sehl·duh·rie	celery [celeriac]
koekje <u>kook</u>·yuh	cookie [biscuit]
koffie <u>kohf</u>·fee	coffee
kokos <u>koa</u>·kohs	coconut
kokosmakroon <u>koa</u>·kohs·maa·kroan	coconut macaroon
komijn koa·<u>mien</u>	cumin
komijnekaas koa·<u>mie</u>·nuh·kaas	cheese with cumin seeds
komkommer kohm·<u>kohm</u>·muhr	cucumber
komkommersalade kohm·<u>kohm</u>·muhr·saa·<u>laa</u>·duh	cucumber salad
konijn koa·<u>nien</u>	rabbit
koninginnensoep <u>koa</u>·nihng·<u>ihn</u>·uhn·soop	cream of chicken
kool koal	cabbage
koolrabi <u>koal</u>·raa·bee	kohlrabi
koolsla <u>koal</u>·slaa	coleslaw
koolzuurhoudend (water) <u>koal</u>·zewr·<u>how</u>·duhnt (<u>vaa</u>·tuhr)	sparkling (water)
koolzuurvrij (water) <u>koal</u>·zewr·frie (<u>vaa</u>·tuhr)	still (water)
koriander koh·ree·<u>ahn</u>·duhr	cilantro [coriander]
korstdeeg <u>kohrst</u>·daykh	puff pastry
kort gebakken kohrt khuh·<u>bah</u>·kuhn	rare
kotelet koa·tuh·<u>leht</u>	chop, cutlet
krab krap	crab
kreeft krayft	lobster
krentenbol <u>krehn</u>·tuhn·bohl	currant bun
krentenbrood <u>krehn</u>·tuhn·broat	currant bread

kroepoek kroo·pook — shrimp [prawn] crackers

kroket kroa·keht — croquettes

kropsla krohp·slaa — cabbage lettuce

kruiden kraw·duhn — herbs

kruidnagel krawt·naa·khuhl — clove

kruisbes kraws·behs — gooseberry

kwarktaart kvahrk·taart — light cheesecake

kwartelvlees kvahr·tuhl·flays — quail

kweegelei kvay·zhuh·lei — quince jelly

kwets kvehts — blue plum

lamsbout lahms·bowt — leg of lamb

lamsstoofschotel lahms·stoaf·skhoa·tuhl — lamb stew

lamsvlees lahms·flays — lamb

lamszadel lahms·zaa·duhl — saddle (lamb)

laurierblad low·reer·blaht — bay leaf

lekkerbekje leh·kuhr·behk·yuh — breaded fillet of haddock

lendebiefstuk lehn·duh·beef·stuhk — fillet, rump steak

lendevlees lehn·duh·flays — loin meat

lente-uitje lehn·tuh·aw·tyuh — spring onion

lever lay·fuhr — liver

likeur lee·kur — liqueur

limoen lee·moon — lime

limoensap lee·moon·sahp — lime juice

limonade lee·moa·naa·duh — lemonade

limonadesiroop lee·moa·naa·duh·see·roap — fruit drink concentrate of various flavors

linze <u>lihn</u>·zuh	lentil
loempia <u>loom</u>·pee·yaa	spring roll
lofsalade <u>lohf</u>·sah·laa·duh	salad of raw chicory rings
lopend buffet <u>loa</u>·puhnt bew·<u>feht</u>	buffet
maïs <u>mah</u>·ees	sweet corn
makreel <u>maa</u>·krayl	mackerel
mandarijn mahn·daa·<u>rien</u>	tangerine
marmelade mahr·muh·<u>laa</u>·duh	marmalade
marsepein mahr·suh·<u>pien</u>	marzipan
mayonaise maa·yoh·<u>neh</u>·suh	mayonnaise
melk mehlk	milk
meloen muh·<u>loon</u>	melon
metworst <u>meht</u>·vohrst	spicy sausage
mie mee	noodles
mierikswortel <u>mee</u>·rihks·wohr·tuhl	horseradish
milkshake <u>mihlk</u>·shayk	milk shake
mineraalwater mee·nuh·<u>raal</u>·vaa·tuhr	mineral water
moerbei <u>moor</u>·bie	mulberry
moorkop <u>mohr</u>·kohp	chocolate éclair
mossel <u>moh</u>·suhl	mussel
mosterd <u>mohs</u>·tuhrt	mustard
mousserende wijn moo·<u>say</u>·ruhn·duh vien	sparkling wine
mul muhl	red mullet
munt muhnt	mint
muntthee <u>muhnt</u>·tay	mint tea

nasi goreng <u>naa</u>·see <u>khoa</u>·rehng — Indonesian fried rice with spices, meat and egg

nectarine nehk·taa·<u>ree</u>·nuh — nectarine

niertjes <u>neer</u>·tyuhs — kidneys

nieuwe haring <u>neeew</u>·vuh <u>haa</u>·rihng — freshly caught, salt-cured herring

noga <u>noa</u>·gaa — nougat

nootmuskaat <u>noat</u>·muhs·kaat — nutmeg

octopus <u>ohk</u>·toa·puhs — octopus

oester <u>oos</u>·tuhr — oyster

oesterzwam <u>oos</u>·tuhr·zwahm — oyster mushroom

olie en azijn <u>oa</u>·lee ehn aa·<u>zien</u> — oil and vinegar

olijf oa·<u>lief</u> — olive

omelet <u>oh</u>·muh·leht — omelet

ossenhaas <u>oh</u>·suhn·haas — tenderloin (beef)

ossenstaartsoep <u>oh</u>·suhn·staart·<u>soop</u> — oxtail soup

oude kaas <u>ow</u>·duh kaas — hard cheese

paddenstoel <u>pah</u>·duhn·stool — field mushroom

paling <u>paa</u>·lihng — eel

pannenkoek <u>pah</u>·nuhn·kook — pancake

paprika <u>paa</u>·pree·kaa — (sweet) pepper

parelhoen <u>paa</u>·ruhl·hoon — guinea fowl

passievrucht <u>pah</u>·see·fruhkht — passion fruit

pasta <u>pahs</u>·taa — pasta

pastei pahs·<u>tie</u> — pie

pasteideeg pahs·<u>tie</u>·daykh — pastry

pasteitje (vol-au-vent) pahs·<u>tie</u>·tyuh (<u>fohl</u>·oa·fahn) — pastry filled with meat or fish

pastinaak pahs·tee·<u>naak</u>	parsnips
patat paa·<u>taht</u>	French fries [chips]
paté paa·<u>tay</u>	paté
patrijs paa·<u>tries</u>	partridge
peer payr	pear
pekelvlees <u>pay</u>·kuhl·flays	sliced, salted meat
pens pehns	tripe
peper <u>pay</u>·puhr	black pepper
pepernoten <u>pay</u>·puhr·noa·tuhn	gingerbread nuts
perzik <u>pehr</u>·zihk	peach
peterselie <u>pay</u>·tuhr·say·lee	parsley
peultjes <u>pul</u>·tyuhs	sugar peas
piepkuiken <u>peep</u>·kaw·kuhn	spring chicken
pikant pee·<u>kahnt</u>	hot (spicy)
pikant worstje pee·<u>kahnt</u> <u>vohrst</u>·yuh	spicy sausage
pils pihls	lager
pinda <u>pihn</u>·daa	peanut
pindasaus <u>pihn</u>·daa·sows	peanut sauce
pitabroodje <u>pee</u>·taa·broat·<u>yuh</u>	pita bread
plaatselijke specialiteit <u>plaats</u>·uh·luh·kuh <u>spay</u>·shaa·lee·<u>tiet</u>	local speciality
poffertje <u>poh</u>·fuhr·tyuh	tiny pancake
pompoen pohm·<u>poon</u>	pumpkin
portie <u>pohr</u>·see	portion
prei prie	leek
prinsessenboon prihn·<u>seh</u>·suhn·<u>boan</u>	haricot bean
pruim prawm	plum
raap raap	turnip

rabarber raa·<u>bahr</u>·buhr	rhubarb
radijs raa·<u>dies</u>	radish
rammenas <u>rah</u>·muh·nahs	winter radish
rauw row	raw
reebout <u>ray</u>·bowt	venison
ribstuk <u>rihp</u>·stuhk	rib
rijst riest	rice
rijstebrij <u>ries</u>·tuh·<u>brie</u>	rice pudding
risotto ree·<u>soh</u>·toa	risotto
rivierkreeft ree·<u>feer</u>·krayft	crayfish
rode kool <u>roa</u>·duh koal	red cabbage
rode paprika <u>roa</u>·duh <u>paa</u>·pree·kaa	sweet red pepper
rode peper <u>roa</u>·duh <u>pay</u>·puhr	chili pepper
roerei <u>roor</u>·ie	scrambled egg
rog rohkh	ray
roggebrood <u>roh</u>·khuh·broat	rye bread
rollade roh·<u>laa</u>·duh	meat roll
romig <u>roa</u>·mihkh	creamy
rookvlees <u>roak</u>·flays	smoked or smoke-dried beef
room roam	cream
roomijs <u>roam</u>·ies	ice cream
roomsoep <u>roam</u>·soop	cream soup
rosbief <u>rohs</u>·beef	roast beef
rozemarijn <u>roa</u>·zuh·maa·<u>rijn</u>	rosemary
rozijn roa·<u>zien</u>	raisin
rum ruhm	rum
rundvlees <u>ruhnt</u>·flays	beef

Russisch ei ruh·sees ie	hard-boiled egg filled with mayonnaise, garnished with fish and salad
saffraan sah·fraan	saffron
sajur lodeh saa·yoor loa·deh	Indonesian vegetable dish
salade saa·laa·duh	salad
salie saa·lee	sage
sandwich sehnt·wihtsh	sandwich
sap sahp	juice
sardientje sahr·deen·tyuh	sardine
saté saa·tay	meat on skewers
saucijzenbroodje sow·sie·zuhn·broat·yuh	sausage roll
saucijs sow·sies	sausage
saus sows	sauce
savooiekool saa·voa·yuh·koal	savoy cabbage
schaaldieren skhaal·dee·ruhn	shellfish
schapenkaas skhaa·puhn·kaas	ewe's milk cheese
schapenvlees skhaa·puhn·flays	mutton
schelpdier skhehlp·deer	shellfish, clam
schelvis skhehl·fihs	haddock
schenkel skhehn·kuhl	shank (top of leg)
schimmelkaas skhih·muhl·kaas	blue cheese
schnitzel shniht·zuhl	veal or pork cutlet
schol skhohl	plaice
schuimgebakje skhawm·khuh·bahk·yuh	meringue
selderij sehl·duh·rie	celery
sinaasappel see·naas·ah·puhl	orange

sinaasappelsap <u>see</u>·naas·ah·puhl·sahp	orange juice
siroop see·<u>roap</u>	syrup
sjalotten shaa·<u>loh</u>·tuhn	shallots
sla slaa	lettuce
slagroom <u>slakh</u>·roam	sweet whipped cream
slak <u>slahk</u>	snail
slasaus <u>slaa</u>·sows	salad dressing
snijbonen <u>snie</u>·boa·nuhn	sliced green beans
snoepje <u>snoop</u>·yuh	candy [sweet]
soep soop	soup
soesje <u>soos</u>·yuh	pastry filled with whipped cream
specerijen spay·suh·<u>rie</u>·yuhn	spices
speclalltelten van de chef-kok <u>spay</u>·shaa·lee·<u>tie</u>·tuhn fahn duh <u>shehf</u>·kohk	speclalltlles of the house
speculaas <u>spay</u>·kew·laas	spiced cookie [biscuit]
speenvarken <u>spayn</u>·fahr·kuhn	suckling pig
spek spehk	bacon
spekpannenkoek spehk·<u>pah</u>·nuhn·kook	bacon pancake
sperzieboon <u>spehr</u>·see·boan	green bean
spiegelei <u>spee</u>·khuhl·ie	fried egg
spijkerrog <u>spie</u>·kuhr·rohkh	skate (fish)
spinazie spee·<u>naa</u>·zee	spinach
spitskool <u>spihts</u>·koal	type of cabbage
sprits sprihts	Dutch shortbread
sprot sproht	sprat (fish)
spruitje <u>spraw</u>·tyuh	Brussel sprout

stamppot <u>stahm</u>·poht	one-pan dish with vegetables and mashed potatoes
sterk stehrk	strong (flavor)
stervrucht <u>stehr</u>·fruhkht	star fruit
stokbrood <u>stohk</u>·broat	French-style bread
stokvisschotel <u>stohk</u>·fihs·<u>skhoa</u>·tuhl	oven stew of dried cod
stoofschotel <u>stoaf</u>·skhoa·tuhl	casserole, stew
stroop stroap	molasses
stroopwafel <u>stroap</u>·vaa·fuhl	two waffles with syrup in between them
suiker <u>saw</u>·kuhr	sugar
suikerglazuur <u>saw</u>·kuhr·<u>khlaa</u>·zewr	icing
sultanarozijn suhl·<u>taa</u>·naa·roa·<u>zien</u>	sultana raisin
taart taart	tart
taartje <u>taart</u>·yuh	tartlette
tafelwijn <u>taa</u>·fuhl·<u>vien</u>	table wine
tafelzuur <u>taa</u>·fuhl·<u>zewr</u>	pickle
tahoe/tofoe <u>taa</u>·hoo/<u>toa</u>·few	tofu
tarbot tahr·<u>boa</u>	turbot
tartaartje tahr·<u>taar</u>·tyuh	ground steak
taugé <u>tow</u>·gay	bean sprouts
thee tay	tea
tijm tiem	thyme
toast toast	toast
toeristenmenu too·<u>rihs</u>·tuhn·muh·<u>new</u>	tourist menu
tomaat toa·<u>maat</u>	tomato
tomatenketchup toa·<u>maa</u>·tuhn·keht·shuhp	ketchup
tomatensaus toa·<u>maa</u>·tuhn·sows	tomato sauce

tomatensoep toa·<u>maa</u>·tuhn·soop	tomato soup
tompoes tohm·<u>poos</u>	cake slice with custard filling
tong tohng	tongue, sole
tonic <u>toh</u>·nihk	tonic water
tonijn toa·<u>nien</u>	tuna
tosti <u>tohs</u>·tee	toasted sandwich
tournedos toor·<u>nay</u>·dohs	fillet steak
truffel <u>truh</u>·fuhl	truffle
tuinboon <u>tawn</u>·boan	broad bean
tuinkers <u>tawn</u>·kehrs	cress
tulband <u>tuhl</u>·bahnd	turban-shaped fruit cake
ui aw	onion
uiensoep <u>aw</u>·yuhn·soop	onion soup
uitsmijter <u>awt</u>·smie·tuhr	snack of bread, ham and fried eggs
vanille vaa·<u>nee</u>·yuh	vanilla
varkenshaas <u>fahr</u>·kuhns·haas	tenderloin (pork)
varkenskotelet <u>fahr</u>·kuhns·koa·tuh·<u>leht</u>	pork chop
varkenspootjes <u>fahr</u>·kuhns·poat·yuhs	pigs' feet
varkensvlees <u>fahr</u>·kuhns·flays	pork
varkensworstje <u>fahr</u>·kuhns·<u>vohrst</u>·yuh	pork sausage
veenbes <u>fayn</u>·behs	cranberry
venkel <u>fehn</u>·kuhl	fennel
vermicellisoep <u>fehr</u>·mee·<u>seh</u>·lee·soep	clear noodle soup
vermout fuhr·<u>mowt</u>	vermouth
vers fruit fehrs frawt	fresh fruit
verse kwark <u>fehr</u>·suh kvahrk	fresh-curd cheese

vijg fiekh	fig
vinaigrette fih·nuh·<u>kreht</u>	vinaigrette
vis fihs	fish
vispastei <u>fihs</u>·pahs·<u>tie</u>	chopped fish in a pastry shell
vissoep <u>fihs</u>·soop	fish soup
visstick <u>fihs</u>·stihk	fish stick
vla flaa	custard
vlees flays	meat (general)
vleesbouillon <u>flays</u>·boo·<u>yohn</u>	meat broth
vleespastei <u>flays</u>·pahs·<u>tie</u>	chopped meat in a pastry shell
volkorenmeel fohl·<u>koa</u>·ruhn·mayl	wholewheat flour
voorn foarn	rock-bass (fish)
vruchtendrank <u>fruhkh</u>·tuhn·drahngk	fruit drink
vruchtensap <u>fruhkh</u>·tuhn·sahp	fruit juice
vruchtenvlaai <u>fruhkh</u>·tuhn·flaai	Limburg fruit flan
wafel <u>vaa</u>·fuhl	waffle
walnoot <u>vahl</u>·noat	walnut
warme chocolademelk <u>vahr</u>·muh shoa·koa·<u>laa</u>·duh·mehlk	hot chocolate
waterkastanje <u>vaa</u>·tuhr·kahs·<u>tahn</u>·yuh	water chestnut
waterkers <u>vaa</u>·tuhr·kehrs	watercress
watermeloen <u>vaa</u>·tuhr·muh·<u>loon</u>	watermelon
wentelteefje <u>vehn</u>·tuhl·tayf·yuh	French toast
wienerschnitzel <u>vee</u>·nuhr <u>shniht</u>·suhl	breaded veal slices
wijn vien	wine
wijting <u>vie</u>·tihng	whiting
wild vihlt	game

wild zwijn vihlt zvien — wild boar

wilde eend <u>vihl</u>·duh aynt — wild duck

witlof <u>viht</u>·lohf — chicory

witlofsalade <u>viht</u>·lohf·saa·laa·duh — chicory salad

witte asperge (met saus) <u>vih</u>·tuh <u>ah</u>·spehr·zhuh (meht sows) — white asparagus (with sauce)

witte bonen <u>vih</u>·tuh <u>boa</u>·nuhn — haricot beans

witte druif <u>vih</u>·tuh drawf — green grape

witte kool <u>vih</u>·tuh koal — white cabbage

witte saus <u>vih</u>·tuh sows — white sauce

wodka <u>vohd</u>·kaa — vodka

worstje <u>vohrst</u>·yuh — sausage

wortel <u>vohr</u>·tuhls — carrot

wortelsalade <u>vohr</u>·tuhl·saa·<u>laa</u>·duh — raw grated carrot

yoghurt <u>yoh</u>·khuhrt — yogurt

zacht gekookt zahkht khuh·<u>koakt</u> — soft-boiled

zachte kaas <u>zahkh</u>·tuh kaas — soft cheese

zalm zahlm — salmon

zandgebak <u>zahnd</u>·khuh·bahk — shortbread, shortcake

zeebaars <u>zay</u>·baars — sea bass

zeebliek <u>zay</u>·bleek — whitebait

zeebrasem <u>zay</u>·braa·suhm — sea bream

zeeduivel <u>zay</u>·daw·fuhl — monkfish

zeekat <u>zay</u>·kaht — cuttlefish

zeepaling <u>zay</u>·paa·lihng — conger eel

zoetzure saus zoot·<u>zew</u>·ruh sows — sweet and sour sauce

zoetje <u>zoot</u>·yuh — sweetener

zoetwatervis zoot·<u>vaa</u>·tuhr·fihs — freshwater fish

zout zowt	salt
zoutwatervis zowt·<u>vaa</u>·tuhr·fihs	saltwater fish
zure bom <u>zew</u>·ruh bohm	large gherkin
zure haring <u>zew</u>·ruh <u>haa</u>·rihng	pickled herring [rollmops]
zuring <u>zew</u>·rihng	sorrel
zuurkool <u>zewr</u>·koal	sauerkraut
zwaardvis <u>zvaart</u>·fihs	swordfish
zwarte bes <u>zvahr</u>·tuh <u>behs</u>	black currant

▼ *People*

Talking

Essential

Hello./Hi!	**Dag./Hallo!** dakh/hah·loa
How are you?	**Hoe gaat het met u?** hoo khaat heht meht ew
Fine, thanks.	**Prima, dank u.** pree·maa dangk ew
Excuse me! (to a man/woman)	**Meneer/Mevrouw!** muh·nayr/muh·frow
Do you speak English?	**Spreekt u Engels?** spraykt ew ehng·uhls
What's your name?	**Hoe heet u?** hoo hayt ew
My name is…	**Mijn naam is…** mien naam ihs…
Nice to meet you.	**Aangenaam.** aan·khuh·naam
Where are you from?	**Waar komt u vandaan?** vaar kohmt ew fahn·daan
I'm from the U.S./U.K.	**Ik kom uit de Verenigde Staten/ Groot-Brittannië.** ihk kohm awt duh fuhr·ay·nihkh·duh staa·tuhn/ khroat·brih·tah·nee·yuh
What do you do?	**Wat doet u in het dagelijks leven?** vaht doot ew ihn heht daa·khuh·luks lay·fuhn
I work for…	**Ik werk bij…** ihk vehrk bie…
I'm a student.	**Ik ben student.** ihk behn stew·dehnt
I'm retired.	**Ik ben met pensioen.** ihk behn meht pehn·shoon
Do you like…?	**Houdt u van…?** howt ew fahn…
Goodbye.	**Dag.** dakh
See you later.	**Tot ziens.** toht zeens

When addressing people you don't know, use **u** (formal you) or **meneer** (sir) and **mevrouw** (ma'am or madam), particularly with strangers and older people. It is impolite to address someone with the familiar **jij** and **je** (**jullie**, in the plural) until invited to do so.

Communication Difficulties

Do you speak English? **Spreekt u Engels?** spraykt ew <u>ehng</u>·uhls

Does anyone here speak English? **Is er hier iemand die Engels spreekt?** ihs ehr heer <u>ee</u>·mahnt dee <u>ehng</u>·uhls spraykt

I don't speak Dutch. **Ik spreek geen Nederlands.** ihk sprayk khayn <u>nay</u>·duhr·lahnts

I don't speak much Dutch. **Ik spreek maar weinig Nederlands.** ihk sprayk maar <u>vie</u>·nihkh <u>nay</u>·duhr·lahnts

Can you speak more slowly? **Kunt u iets langzamer spreken?** kuhnt ew eets <u>lahng</u>·zaa·muhr <u>spray</u>·kuhn

Can you repeat that? **Kunt u dat herhalen?** kuhnt ew daht hehr·<u>haa</u>·luhn

Excuse me? **Pardon?** pahr·<u>dohn</u>

What was that? **Wat zegt u?** vaht zehkht ew

Can you write it down? **Kunt u het opschrijven?** kuhnt ew heht ohp·<u>skhrie</u>·fuhn

Can you translate this for me? **Kunt u dit voor mij vertalen?** kuhnt ew diht foar mie fuhr·<u>taa</u>·luhn

What does this mean? **Wat betekent dit?** vaht buh·<u>tay</u>·kuhnt diht

I (don't) understand. **Ik begrijp het (niet).** ihk buh·<u>khrayp</u> heht (neet)

Do you understand? **Begrijpt u het?** buh·<u>khraypt</u> ew heht

Ik spreek slechts weinig Engels. ihk sprayk slehkhts <u>vie</u>·nihkh <u>ehng</u>·uhls	I only speak a little English.
Ik spreek geen Engels. ihk sprayk khayn <u>ehng</u>·uhls	I don't speak English.

Making Friends

Hello./Hi!	**Dag./Hallo!** dakh/hah·<u>loa</u>
Good morning.	**Goedemorgen.** <u>khoo</u>·duh·<u>mohr</u>·khuhn
Good afternoon.	**Goedemiddag.** <u>khoo</u>·duh·<u>mih</u>·dahkh
Good evening.	**Goedenavond.** <u>khoo</u>·duh·<u>naa</u>·fohnt
My name is…	**Mijn naam is…** mien naam ihs…
What's your name?	**Hoe heet u?** hoo hayt ew
I'd like to introduce you to…	**Ik wil u graag voorstellen aan…** ihk vihl ew khraakh <u>foar</u>·steh·luhn aan…
Nice to meet you.	**Aangenaam.** <u>aan</u>·khuh·naam
How are you?	**Hoe gaat het met u?** hoo khaat heht meht ew
Fine, thanks.	**Prima, dank u.** <u>pree</u>·ma dangk ew
And you?	**En met u?** en meht ew

i In the Netherlands, upon meeting, it is customary to shake hands and to use a greeting appropriate for the time of day. Close friends may kiss cheeks (left, right, left) and say **Hoe gaat het?** (How are you?) or **Alles goed?** (Is everything alright?). You'll find surnames are used more frequently than first names, even when answering the phone. When entering a store, greet the shop attendant by saying **goedemorgen, goedemiddag,** or **goedenavond** (good morning, good afternoon, good evening). When leaving you can say **dag** or **tot ziens** (good day or goodbye).

Travel Talk ——————————

I'm here…	**Ik ben hier…** ihk behn heer…
– on business	**– voor zaken** foar <u>zaa</u>·kuhn
– on vacation [holiday]	**– met vakantie** meht faa·<u>kahn</u>·see
– studying	**– voor studie** foar <u>stew</u>·dee
I'm staying for…	**Ik blijf…** ihk blief…
I've been here…	**Ik ben hier al…** ihk behn heer ahl…
– a day	**– een dag** uhn dahkh
– a week	**– een week** uhn vayk
– a month	**– een maand** uhn maant

▶For numbers, see page 158.

| Where are you from? | **Waar komt u vandaan?** vaar kohmt cw fahn·<u>daan</u> |
| I'm from… | **Ik kom uit…** ihk kohm awt… |

Relationships

Who are you with?	**Met wie bent u?** meht vee behnt ew
I'm on my own.	**Ik ben in mijn eentje.** Ihk behn ihn mien ayn·tyuh
I'm with...	**Ik ben met...** ihk behn meht...
– my *husband/wife*	**– mijn *man/vrouw*** mien *mahn/frow*
– my *boyfriend/ girlfriend*	**– mijn *vriend/vriendin*** mien *freent/freen·dihn*
– a friend	**– een vriend** uhn freent
– a colleague	**– een collega** uhn koh·lay·khaa
When's your birthday?	**Wanneer bent u jarig?** vah·nayr behnt ew yaa·rihk
How old are you?	**Hoe oud bent u?** hoo owt behnt ew
I'm...	**Ik ben...** ihk behn...

▶ For numbers, see page 158.

Are you married?	**Bent u getrouwd?** behnt ew khuh·trowt
I'm...	**Ik ben...** ihk behn...
– single	**– ongetrouwd** ohn·khuh·trowt
– married	**– getrouwd** khuh·trowt
– divorced	**– gescheiden** khuh·skhie·duhn
– separated	**– uit elkaar** awt ehl·kaar
I'm in a relationship.	**Ik heb een relatie.** ihk hehp uhn ray·laat·see
I'm widowed.	**Ik ben *weduwnaar♂/weduwe♀*.** ihk behn vay·dew·naar♂ /vay·dew·uh♀
Do you have *children/ grandchildren*?	**Heeft u *kinderen/kleinkinderen*?** hayft ew kihn·duh·ruhn/klien·kihn·duh·ruhn

104

Work and School

What do you do?	**Wat doet u in het dagelijks leven?** vaht doot ew ihn heht <u>daa</u>·khuh·luks <u>lay</u>·fuhn
What are you studying?	**Wat studeert u?** vaht stew·<u>dayrt</u> ew
I'm studying…	**Ik studeer…** ihk stew·<u>dayr</u>…
Who do you work for?	**Voor wie werkt u?** foar vee vehrkt ew
I work for…	**Ik werk voor…** ihk vehrk foar…
Here's my business card.	**Hier is mijn visitekaartje.** heer ihs mien fee·<u>zee</u>·tuh·kaart·yuh

▶ For business travel, see page 137.

Weather

What's the weather forecast?	**Wat is het weerbericht?** vaht ihs heht <u>vayr</u>·buh·rIhkht
What *beautiful/terrible* weather!	**Wat een *mooi/vreselijk* weer!** vaht uhn *moay/<u>fray</u>·suh·luhk* vayr
It's *cool/warm*.	**Het is *koel/warm*.** heht ihs *kool/vahrm*
It's *rainy/sunny*.	**Het is *regenachtig/zonnig*.** heht ihs *<u>ray</u>·khuhn·ahkh·tikh/<u>zoh</u>·nihkh*
It's *snowy/icy*.	**Het *sneeuwt/vriest*.** heht *snaywt/freest*
Do I need *a jacket/ an umbrella*?	**Moet ik een *jas/paraplu* meenemen?** moot ihk uhn *jahs/paa·raa·<u>plew</u>* <u>may</u>·nay·muhn

▶ For temperature, see page 164.

Romance

Essential

Would you like to go out for a *drink/meal*?	**Heb je zin *om iets te gaan drinken/uit eten te gaan*?** hehp yuh zihn ohm eets tuh gaan drihn·kuhn/awt ay·tuhn tuh gaan
What are your plans for *tonight/tomorrow*?	**Wat zijn je plannen voor *vanavond/morgen*?** vaht zien yuh plah·nuhn foar fah·naa·fohnt/mohr·khuhn
Can I have your phone number?	**Mag ik je telefoonnummer?** mahkh ihk yuh tay·luh·foan·nuh·muhr
Can I join you?	**Mag ik bij je komen zitten?** mahkh ihk bie yuh koa·muhn zih·tuhn
Can I buy you a drink?	**Wil je iets van me drinken?** vihl yuh eets fahn muh drihng·kuhn
I like you.	**Ik mag je graag.** ihk mahkh yuh khraakh
I love you.	**Ik hou van je.** ihk how fahn yuh

Making Plans

Would you like to go out for coffee?	**Wil je ergens koffie gaan drinken?** vihl yuh ehr·khuhns koh·fee khaan drihng·kuhn
What are your plans for…?	**Wat zijn je plannen voor…?** vaht zien yuh plah·nuhn foar…
– tonight	**– vanavond** fah·naa·fohnt
– tomorrow	**– morgen** mohr·khuhn
– this weekend	**– dit weekend** diht vee·kehnt
Where would you like to go?	**Waar wil je naartoe?** vaar vihl yuh naar too

Throughout this section, the informal you is applied in Dutch.

I'd like to go to…	**Ik wil graag naar…** ihk vihl khraakh naar…
Do you like…?	**Hou je van…?** how yuh fahn…
Can I have your *number/e-mail*?	**Mag ik je *nummer/e-mailadres*?** mahkh ihk yuh _nuh_·muhr/_ee_·mayl·aa·_drehs_

▶ For e-mail and phone, see page 45.

Pick-up [Chat-up] Lines

Can I join you?	**Mag ik bij je komen zitten?** mahkh ihk bie yuh _koa_·muhn _zih_·tuhn
You're very attractive.	**Je ziet er fantastisch uit.** yuh zeet ehr fahn·_tahs_·tees awt
Shall we go somewhere quieter?	**Zullen we een rustig plekje opzoeken?** _zuh_·luhn vuh uhn _ruhs_·tikh _plehk_·yuh _ohp_·zoo·kuhn

Accepting and Rejecting

| Thank you. I'd love to. | **Dank je. Dat zou erg leuk zijn.** dangk yuh daht zow ehrkh luk zien |
| Where should we meet? | **Waar zullen we elkaar ontmoeten?** vaar _zuh_·luhn vuh ehl·_kaar_ ohnt·_moo_·tuhn |

I'll meet you at *the bar/your hotel.*	**Laten we in *de bar/jouw hotel* afspreken.** laa·tuhn vuh ihn *duh bahr/yow hoa·tehl* ahf·spray·kuhn
I'll come by at...	**Ik haal je om...uur op.** ihk haal yuh ohm... uwr ohp
Thank you, but I'm busy.	**Dank je, maar ik heb het te druk.** dangk yuh maar ihk hehp heht tuh druhk
I'm not interested.	**Ik heb geen interesse.** ihk hehp khayn ihn·tuh·reh·suh
Leave me alone, please.	**Laat me alstublieft met rust.** laat muh ahls·tew·bleeft meht ruhst
Stop bothering me.	**Blijf me niet steeds lastig vallen.** blief muh neet stayts lahs·tihkh fah·luhn

Getting Physical

Can I *hug/kiss* you?	**Mag ik je *omhelzen/zoenen?*** mahkh ihk yuh *ohm·hehl·zuhn/zoo·nuhn*
Yes.	**Ja.** yaa
No.	**Nee.** nay
Stop!	**Stop!** stohp

Sexual Preferences

Are you gay?	**Ben je homo♂/lesbisch♀?** behn yuh hoa·moa♂/lehs·bees♀
I'm...	**Ik ben...** ihk behn...
– heterosexual	**– hetero** hay·tuh·roa
– homosexual	**– homo** hoa·moa
– bisexual	**– biseksueel** bee·sehk·sew·ayl

▼ Fun

Sightseeing

Essential

Where's the tourist information office?	**Waar is het VVV-kantoor?** vaar ihs heht vay·vay·<u>vay</u>·kahn·<u>toar</u>
What are the main points of interest?	**Wat zijn de bezienswaardigheden?** vaht zien duh buh·zeens·<u>waar</u>·dihkh·hay·duhn
Do you have tours in English?	**Verzorgt u excursies in het Engels?** fuhr·<u>zohrkht</u> ew ehks·<u>kuhr</u>·sees ihn heht <u>ehng</u>·uhls
Can I have a *map/ guide* please?	**Mag ik een *kaart/gids*, alstublieft?** mahkh ihk uhn *kaart/<u>khihts</u>* ahls·tew·<u>bleeft</u>

Tourist Information Office ───────

Do you have any information on…?	**Heeft u informatie over…?** hayft ew ihn·fohr·<u>maat</u>·see <u>oa</u>·fuhr…
Can you recommend…?	**Kunt u…aanbevelen?** kuhnt ew… <u>aan</u>·buh·fay·luhn
– a boat trip	**– een rondvaart** uhn <u>rohnt</u>·faart
– an excursion	**– een excursie** uhn eks·<u>kuhr</u>·see
– a sightseeing tour	**– een toeristische rondrit** uhn too·<u>rihs</u>·tee·suh <u>rohnt</u>·riht

> *i* **VVV, Vereniging voor Vreemdelingenverkeer** (tourist information offices), are located throughout the Netherlands, and offer a number of services such as assisting in travel arrangements, providing information about attractions and cultural events, booking tickets and making reservations.

Tours

I'd like to go on the tour to…	**Ik wil graag de excursie doen naar…** ihk vihl khraakh duh ehks·<u>kuhr</u>·see doon naar…
Are there tours in English?	**Zijn er excursies in het Engels?** zien ehr ehks·<u>kuhr</u>·sees ihn heht <u>ehng</u>·uhls
What time do we *leave/return*?	**Hoe laat *vertrekken we/komen we terug*?** hoo laat *fuhr·<u>treh</u>·kuhn vuh/<u>koa</u>·muhn vuh truhkh*
Can we stop here…?	**Kunnen we hier stoppen…?** <u>kuh</u>·nuhn vuh heer <u>stoh</u>·puhn…
– to take photographs	**– om foto's te nemen** ohm <u>foa</u>·toas tuh <u>nay</u>·muhn
– to buy souvenirs	**– om souvenirs te kopen** ohm soo·fuh·<u>neers</u> tuh <u>koa</u>·puhn
– to use the restrooms [toilets]	**– om naar het toilet te gaan** ohm naar heht tvaa·<u>leht</u> tuh khaan
Is there access for the disabled?	**Is het toegankelijk voor gehandicapten?** ihs heht too·<u>khahn</u>·kuh·luhk foar khuh·<u>hehn</u>·dee·kehp·tuhn

▶For ticketing, see page 19.

Sights

Where *is/are*...?	**Waar *is/zijn*...?** vaar *ihs/zien*...
– the botanical garden	**– de botanische tuin** duh boa·<u>taa</u>·nee·suh tawn
– the castle	**– het kasteel** heht kahs·<u>tayl</u>
– the downtown area	**– het stadscentrum** heht <u>staht</u>·sehn·truhm
– the fountain	**– de fontein** duh fohn·<u>tien</u>
– the library	**– de bibliotheek** duh bee·blee·oa·<u>tayk</u>
– the market	**– de markt** duh mahrkt
– the museum	**– het museum** heht mew·<u>zay</u>·uhm
– the old town	**– het oude stadsgedeelte** heht <u>ow</u>·duh <u>stahts</u>·khuh·<u>dayl</u>·tuh
– the palace	**– het paleis** heht paa·<u>lies</u>
– the park	**– het park** heht pahrk
– the ruins	**– de ruïnes** duh rew·<u>ee</u>·nuhs
– the shopping area	**– de winkels** duh <u>vihn</u>·kuhls
– the town square	**– het stadsplein** heht <u>stahts</u>·plien
Can you show me on the map?	**Kunt u dat op de kaart laten zien?** kuhnt ew daht ohp duh <u>kaart</u> <u>laa</u>·tuhn zeen

▶ For directions, see page 33.

Impressions

It's...	**Het is...** heht ihs...
– beautiful	**– mooi** moay
– boring	**– saai** saay
– interesting	**– interessant** ihn·tuh·reh·<u>sahnt</u>
– romantic	**– romantisch** roa·<u>mahn</u>·tees
– terrible	**– vreselijk** <u>fray</u>·suh·luhk
– ugly	**– lelijk** <u>lay</u>·luhk

| I *like/don't like* it. | **Ik vind het *mooi/niet mooi.*** ihk fihnt heht *moay/neet moay* |

Religion

Where's...?	**Waar is...?** vaar ihs...
– the church	**– de kerk** duh kehrk
– the mosque	**– de moskee** duh mohs·kay
– the synagogue	**– de synagoge** duh see·naa·khoa·khuh
– the temple	**– de tempel** duh tehm·puhl
What time is *mass/ the service*?	**Hoe laat is *de mis/dienst*?** hoo laat ihs duh *mihs/deenst*

Shopping

Essential

Where is the *market/ mall [shopping centre]*?	**Waar is *de markt/het winkelcentrum*?** vaar ihs *duh mahrkt/heht vihn·kuhl·sehn·truhm*
I'm just looking.	**Ik kijk alleen.** ihk kiek ah·layn
Can you help me?	**Kunt u me helpen?** kuhnt ew muh hehl·puhn
I'm being helped.	**Ik word al geholpen.** ihk vohrt ahl khuh·hohl·puhn
How much?	**Hoeveel kost het?** hoo·fayl kohst heht
That one.	**Die daar.** dee daar
That's all, thanks.	**Meer niet, dank u.** mayr neet dangk ew
Where do I pay?	**Waar moet ik betalen?** vaar moot ihk buh·taa·luhn

| I'll pay *in cash/by credit card*. | **Ik wil graag *contant/met een creditcard* betalen.** ihk vihl *khraakh kohn·<u>tahnt</u>/meht uhn <u>kreh·diht·kaart</u>* buh·<u>taa</u>·luhn |
| A receipt, please. | **Een kwitantie, alstublieft.** uhn kvee·<u>tahn</u>·see ahls·tew·<u>bleeft</u> |

i Visiting the local markets is a fun and colorful experience. There are large as well as small markets throughout the Netherlands, where you can buy all types of goods: fruit and vegetables, cheese and bread, prepared foods, fabric and clothes, plants and flowers and so on. Some are open daily and others weekly; check with the tourist information office for exact schedules. In general, shops are open from Tuesday–Saturday from 9 a.m. to 5 or 6 p.m. Most are closed on Monday morning and some are open on Sunday with shorter hours. In many large cities, Thursdays are late-night shopping days, with stores remaining open until 9 p.m.

Stores

Where is…?	**Waar is…?** vaar ihs…
– the antiques store	– **de antiekwinkel** duh ahn·<u>teek</u>·vihn·kuhl
– the bakery	– **de bakker** duh <u>bah</u>·kuhr
– the bookstore	– **de boekwinkel** duh <u>book</u>·vihn·kuhl
– the clothing store [clothes shop]	– **de kledingwinkel** duh <u>klay</u>·dihng·vihn·kuhl
– the delicatessen	– **de delicatessenwinkel** duh <u>day</u>·lee·kaa·<u>teh</u>·suhn·<u>vihn</u>·kuhl
– the department store	– **het warenhuis** heht <u>vaa</u>·ruhn·haws
– the health food store	– **de reformwinkel** duh ray·<u>fohrm</u>·vihn·kuhl
– the jeweler	– **de juwelier** duh <u>yew</u>·uh·leer
– the liquor store [off-licence]	– **de slijter** duh <u>slie</u>·tuhr
– the market	– **de markt** duh mahrkt
– the pastry shop	– **de banketbakker** duh bang·<u>keht</u>·bah·kuhr
– the pharmacy [chemist]	– **de apotheek** duh ah·poa·<u>tayk</u>
– the produce [grocery] store	– **de groentenboer** duh <u>khroon</u>·tuh·boor
– the shoe store	– **de schoenenwinkel** duh <u>skhoon</u>·uhn·<u>vihn</u>·kuhl
– the shopping mall [centre]	– **het winkelcentrum** heht <u>vihn</u>·kuhl·<u>sehn</u>·truhm
– the souvenir store	– **de souvenirwinkel** duh soo·vuh·<u>neer</u>·<u>vihn</u>·kuhl
– the supermarket	– **de supermarkt** duh <u>sew</u>·puhr·mahrkt
– the tobacconist	– **de tabakswinkel** duh taa·<u>bahks</u>·<u>vihn</u>·kuhl
– the toy store	– **de speelgoedwinkel** duh <u>spayl</u>·khoot·<u>vihn</u>·kuhl

Services

Can you recommend...?	**Kunt u...aanbevelen?** kuhnt ew... <u>aan</u>·buh·fay·luhn
– a barber	**– een herenkapper** uhn <u>hay</u>·ruhn·<u>kah</u>·puhr
– a dry cleaner	**– een stomerij** uhn <u>stoa</u>·muh·<u>rie</u>
– a hairdresser	**– een dameskapper** uhn <u>daa</u>·muhs·<u>kah</u>·puhr
– a laundromat	**– een wasserette** uhn <u>vah</u>·suh·<u>reh</u>·tuh
– a nail salon	**– een nagelsalon** uhn <u>naa</u>·khuhl·saa·<u>lohn</u>
– a spa	**– een kuuroord** uhn <u>kewr</u>·oart
– a travel agency	**– een reisbureau** uhn <u>ries</u>·bew·<u>roa</u>
Can you...this?	**Kunt u dit...?** kuhnt ew diht...
– alter	**– vermaken** fuhr·<u>maa</u>·kuhn
– dry clean	**– stomen** <u>stoa</u>·muhn
– mend	**– verstellen** fuhr·<u>steh</u>·luhn
– press	**– persen** <u>pehr</u>·suhn
When will it be ready?	**Wanneer is het klaar?** <u>vah</u>·nayr ihs heht klaar

Spa

I'd like...	**Ik wil graag...** ihk vihl khraakh...
– an *eyebrow/bikini* wax	**– een *wenkbrauwwax/bikiniwax*** uhn <u>vehnk</u>·brow·vahks/bee·<u>kee</u>·nee·vahks
– a facial	**– een gezichtsbehandeling** uhn khuh·<u>zihkhts</u>·buh·<u>hahn</u>·duh·lihng
– a *manicure/pedicure*	**– een *manicure/pedicure*** uhn maa·nee·<u>kewr</u>/pay·dee·<u>kewr</u>
– a (sports) massage	**– een (sport)massage** uhn (spohrt)mah·<u>saa</u>·zhuh
Do you do...?	**Biedt u...?** beet ew...
– acupuncture	**– acupunctuur** <u>aa</u>·kew·puhnk·<u>tewr</u>

– aromatherapy	– **aromatherapie** aa·<u>roa</u>·maa·tay·raa·<u>pee</u>
– oxygen treatment	– **zuurstofbehandeling** <u>zewr</u>·stohf·buh·<u>hahn</u>·duh·lihng
Is there a sauna?	**Is er een sauna?** ihs ehr uhn <u>sow</u>·naa

Hair Salon

I'd like...	**Ik wil graag...** ihk vihl khraakh...
– an appointment for *today/tomorrow*	– **een afspraak voor *vandaag/morgen*** uhn <u>ahf</u>·spraak foar *fahn·<u>daakh</u> /<u>mohr</u>·khuhn*
– my hair styled	– **m'n haar laten stylen** muhn haar <u>laa</u>·tuhn <u>stie</u>·luhn
– a haircut	– **geknipt worden** <u>khuh</u>·knihpt <u>vohr</u>·duhn
Don't cut it too short.	**Niet te kort, alstublieft.** neet tuh kohrt ahls·tew·<u>bleeft</u>
Shorter here.	**Hier mag het korter.** heer mahkh heht <u>kohr</u>·tuhr

Sales Help

When does...*open/ close*?	**Hoe laat gaat...*open/dicht*?** hoo laat khaat... <u>oa</u>·puhn/dihkht
Where *is/are*...?	**Waar *is/zijn*...?** vaar *ihs/zien*...
– the cashier [cash desk]	– **de kassa** duh <u>kah</u>·saa
– the escalator	– **de roltrap** duh <u>rohl</u>·trahp
– the elevator [lift]	– **de lift** duh lihft
– the fitting rooms	– **de paskamers** duh <u>pahs</u>·kaa·muhrs
– the store guide [directory]	– **winkelplattegrond** <u>vihn</u>·kuhl·plah·tuh·<u>khrohnt</u>
Can you help me?	**Kunt u me helpen?** kuhnt ew muh <u>hehl</u>·puhn
I'm just looking.	**Ik kijk alleen.** ihk kiek ah·<u>layn</u>

I'm being helped.	**Ik word al geholpen.** ihk vohrt ahl khuh·<u>hohl</u>·puhn
Do you have any...?	**Heeft u ook...?** hayft ew oak...
Can you show me...?	**Kunt u me...laten zien?** kuhnt ew muh... <u>laa</u>·tuhn zeen
Can you *ship/wrap* it?	**Kunt u het *versturen/inpakken?*** kuhnt ew heht *fuhr·<u>stew</u>·ruhn/<u>ihn</u>·pah·kuhn*
How much?	**Hoeveel kost het?** <u>hoo</u>·fayl kohst heht
That's all, thanks.	**Meer niet, dank u.** mayr neet dangk ew

▶ For clothing items, see page 124.

▶ For food items, see page 75.

▶ For souvenirs, see page 120.

You May Hear...

Kan ik u helpen? kahn ihk ew <u>hehl</u>·puhn	Can I help you?
Een ogenblik. uhn <u>oa</u>·khuhn·blihk	One moment.
Wat mag het zijn? vaht mahkh heht zien	What would you like?
Anders nog iets? <u>ahn</u>·duhrs nohkh eets	Anything else?

Preferences

I'd like something...	**Ik wil graag iets...** ihk vihl khraakh eets...
– cheap/expensive	**– goedkoops/duurs** khoot·<u>koaps</u>/dewrs
– larger/smaller	**– groters/kleiners** <u>khroa</u>·tuhrs/<u>klie</u>·nuhrs
– from this region	**– uit deze streek** awt <u>day</u>·zuh strayk
Is it real?	**Is het echt?** ihs heht ehkht
Can you show me *this/that*?	**Kunt u me *dit/dat* laten zien?** kuhnt ew muh *diht/daht* <u>laa</u>·tuhn zeen

118

Decisions

That's not quite what I want.	**Dat is niet helemaal wat ik zoek.** daht ihs neet hay·luh·maal vaht ihk zook
No, I don't like it.	**Nee, ik vind het niet mooi.** nay ihk fihnt heht neet moay
That's too expensive.	**Dat is te duur.** daht ihs tuh dewr
I'd like to think about it.	**Ik wil er nog even over nadenken.** ihk vlhl ehr nokh ay·fuhn oa·fuhr naa·dehn·kuhn
I'll take it.	**Ik neem hem.** ihk naym hehm

Bargaining

That's too much.	**Dat is te veel.** daht ihs tuh fayl
I'll give you…	**Ik kan u…geven.** ihk kahn ew…khay·fuhn
Can you give me a discount?	**Kunt u me korting geven?** kuhnt ew muh kohr·tihng khay·fuhn

▶ For numbers, see page 158.

Paying

How much?	**Hoeveel kost het?** hoo·fayl kohst heht
I'll pay *in cash/by credit card.*	**Ik wil graag *contant/met een creditcard* betalen.** ihk vlhl khraakh *kohn·tahnt/meht uhn kreh·diht·kaart* buh·taa·luhn
Can I have a receipt, please?	**Mag ik een kwitantie, alstublieft?** mahkh ihk uhn kvee·tahn·see ahls·tew·bleeft

You May Hear…

Hoe wilt u betalen? hoo vihlt ew buh·taa·luhn	How are you paying?
Alleen contant geld, alstublieft. ah·layn kohn·tahnt khehlt ahls·tew·bleeft	Cash only, please.

Complaints

I'd like...	**Ik wil graag...** ihk vihl khraakh...
– to exchange this	**– dit ruilen** diht <u>raw</u>·luhn
– to return this	**– dit terugbrengen** diht <u>truhkh</u>·brehng·uhn
– a refund	**– mijn geld terug** mien khehlt truhkh
– to see the manager	**– de manager spreken** duh <u>maa</u>·naa·zhuhr <u>spray</u>·kuhn

Souvenirs

decorative tiles	**siertegels** <u>seer</u>·tay·khuhls
(Gouda) candles	**(Goudse) kaarsen** (<u>khowt</u>·suh) <u>kaar</u>·suhn
cookies [biscuits]	**biscuits** <u>bihs</u>·kvees
bottle of wine	**fles wijn** flehs vien
box of chocolates	**doos bonbons** doas <u>bohn</u>·bohns
cheese	**kaas** kaas
chocolate	**chocolade** <u>shoa</u>·koa·<u>laa</u>·duh
clogs	**klompen** <u>klohm</u>·puhn
Delft blue pottery	**Delfts blauw** dehlfts blow
dolls in local costume	**poppen in klederdracht** <u>poh</u>·puhn ihn <u>klay</u>·duhr·drahkht
Dutch egg liqueur	**advocaat** aht·foa·<u>kaat</u>
Dutch gin	**jenever** yuh·<u>nay</u>·fuhr
key ring	**sleutelring** <u>slu</u>·tuhl·rihng
miniature windmill	**miniatuurmolen** mee·nee·yaa·<u>tewr</u>·<u>moa</u>·luhn
porcelain	**porselein** pohr·suh·<u>lien</u>
postcards	**ansichtkaarten** <u>ahn</u>·sihkht·<u>kaar</u>·tuhn

pottery	**aardewerk** <u>aar</u>·duh·vehrk
souvenir guide	**souvenirgids** soo·fuh·<u>neer</u>·khihts
Can I see *this/that*?	**Mag ik *deze/die* zien?** mahkh ihk <u>day</u>·zuh/ dee zeen
It's the one in the *window/display case.*	**Het is die in *de etalage/de vitrine.*** heht ihs dee ihn duh ay·taa·<u>laa</u>·zhuh/duh fee·<u>tree</u>·nuh
I'd like…	**Ik wil graag…** ihk vihl khraakh…
– a battery	**– een batterij** uhn bah·tuh·<u>rie</u>
– bracelet	**– een armband** uhn <u>ahrm</u>·bahnt
– a brooch	**– een broche** uhn broh·<u>shuh</u>
– earrings	**– oorbellen** <u>oar</u>·beh·luhn
– a necklace	**– een halsketting** uhn <u>hahls</u>·keh·tihng
– a ring	**– een ring** uhn rihng
– a watch	**– een horloge** uhn hohr·<u>loa</u>·zhuh
I'd like…	**Ik wil graag iets…** Ihk vihl khraakh eets…
– copper	**– van koper** fahn <u>koa</u>·puhr
– crystal	**– van kristal** fahn krihs·<u>tahl</u>
– diamond	**– van diamant** fahn dee·yaa·<u>mahnt</u>
– *whIte/yellow* gold	**– van *witgoud/geelgoud*** fahn <u>viht</u>·khowt/ <u>khayl</u>·khowt
– pearls	**– met parels** meht <u>paa</u>·ruhls
– pewter	**– van tin** fahn tihn
– platinum	**– van platina** fahn <u>plaa</u>·tee·naa
– sterling silver	**– sterling zilver** <u>stehr</u>·lihng <u>zihl</u>·fuhr
Is this real?	**Is dit echt?** ihs diht ehkht
Can you engrave it?	**Kunt u het graveren?** kuhnt ew heht khraa·<u>fay</u>·ruhn

i The Dutch are especially famous for their flowers and wooden clogs. Other original souvenirs include Delft blue (those not marked with a D are not genuine) and Makkum pottery, tiles, candles from Gouda, pewter, antiques—check around the Nieuwe Spiegelstraat in Amsterdam—and food items such as cheese (especially from Gouda or Edam), chocolate (Droste™) and cookies (Verkade™). Souvenir shops tend to be expensive, but there are many specialty stores. Look for signs indicating tax-free shopping.

Antiques

How old is this?	**Hoe oud is dit?** hoo owt ihs diht
Will I have problems with customs?	**Krijg ik problemen met de douane?** kriekh ihk proa·<u>blay</u>·muhn meht duh doo·<u>vaa</u>·nuh
Is there a certificate of authenticity?	**Is er een certificaat van echtheid?** ihs ehr uhn <u>sehr</u>·tee·fee·<u>kaat</u> fahn <u>ehkht</u>·hiet

Clothing

I'd like…	**Ik wil graag…** ihk vihl khraakh…
Can I try this on?	**Mag ik dit passen?** mahkh ihk diht <u>pah</u>·suhn
It doesn't fit.	**Het past niet.** heht pahst neet
It's too…	**Het is te…** heht ihs tuh…
– big	**– groot** khroat
– small	**– klein** klien
– short	**– kort** kohrt
– long	**– lang** lahng
Do you have this in size…?	**Heeft u dit in maat…?** hayft ew diht ihn maat…
Do you have this in a *bigger/smaller* size?	**Heeft u dit in een *grotere/kleinere* maat?** hayft ew diht ihn uhn <u>khroa</u>·tuh·ruh/<u>klie</u>·nuh·ruh maat

▶ For numbers, see page 158.

You May See…

HERENKLEDING	men's clothing
DAMESKLEDING	women's clothing
KINDERKLEDING	children's clothing

Color

I'd like something in…	**Ik wil graag iets…** ihk vihl khraakh eets…
– beige	**– in beige** ihn <u>beh</u>·zhuh
– black	**– zwarts** zvahrts
– blue	**– blauws** blows
– brown	**– bruins** brawns
– green	**– groens** khroons

I'd like something in…	**Ik wil graag iets…** ihk vihl khraakh eets…
– gray	– **grijs** khries
– orange	– **oranjes** oa·<u>rahn</u>·yuhs
– pink	– **in roze** ihn <u>roh</u>·zuh
– purple	– **paars** paars
– red	– **roods** roats
– white	– **wits** vihts
– yellow	– **geels** khayls

Clothes and Accessories

backpack	**rugzak** <u>ruhkh</u>·zahk
belt	**riem** reem
bikini	**bikini** bee·<u>kee</u>·nee
blouse	**bloes** bloos
bra	**beha** bay·<u>haa</u>
coat	**jas** yahs
dress	**jurk** yuhrk
hat	**hoed** hoot
jacket	**jasje** <u>yahs</u>·yuh
jeans	**spijkerbroek** <u>spie</u>·kuhr·brook
pajamas	**pyjama** pee·<u>yaa</u>·maa
pants [trousers]	**lange broek** <u>lahng</u>·uh brook
pantyhose [tights]	**panty** <u>pehn</u>·tee
purse [handbag]	**handtas** <u>hahn</u>·tahs
raincoat	**regenjas** <u>ray</u>·khuhn·yahs
scarf	**sjaal** shaal
shirt	**overhemd** ♂ <u>oa</u>·fuhr·hehmt ♂
shorts	**korte broek** <u>kohr</u>·tuh brook

skirt	**rok** rohk
socks	**sokken** <u>soh</u>·kuhn
suit	**pak** pahk
sunglasses	**zonnebril** <u>zoh</u>·nuh·brihl
sweater	**trui** traw
sweatshirt	**sweatshirt** <u>sweht</u>·shuhrt
swimming trunks	**zwembroek** <u>zwehm</u>·brook
swimsuit	**zwempak** <u>zweh</u>m·pahk
T-shirt	**T-shirt** <u>tee</u>·shurt
tie	**stropdas** <u>strohp</u>·dahs
underwear	**slip** ♀ **/onderbroek** ♂ slihp ♀ /<u>ohn</u>·duhr·brook ♂

Fabric

I'd like…	**Ik wil graag iets van…** ihk vihl khraakh eets fahn…
– cotton	**– katoen** kaa·<u>toon</u>
– denim	**– spijkerstof** <u>spie</u>·kuhr·stohf
– lace	**– kant** kahnt
– leather	**– leer** layr
– linen	**– linnen** <u>lih</u>·nuhn
– silk	**– zijde** <u>zie</u>·duh
– wool	**– wol** vohl
Is it machine washable?	**Kan het in de machine worden gewassen?** kahn heht ihn duh mah·<u>shee</u>·nuh <u>vohr</u>·duhn khuh·<u>vahs</u>·suhn

Shoes

I'd like…	**Ik wil graag…** ihk vihl khraakh…
– boots	**– laarzen** <u>laar</u>·zuhn
– loafers	**– mocassins** <u>moh</u>·kah·sihns

I'd like…	**Ik wil graag...** ihk vihl khraakh…
– sandals	**– sandalen** sahn·daa·luhn
– shoes	**– schoenen** skhoo·nuhn
– slippers	**– pantoffels** pahn·toh·fuhls
– sneakers	**– gymschoenen** khihm·skhoo·nuhn
In size…	**In maat...** ihn maat…

▶ For numbers, see page 158.

Sizes

small	**klein** klien
medium	**medium** may·dee·yuhm
large	**groot** khroat
extra large	**extra groot** ehks·traa khroat
petite	**tenger** tehng·uhr
plus size	**extra grote maat** ehks·traa khroa·tuh maat

Newsstand and Tobacconist

Do you sell English-language *books/newspapers*?	**Verkoopt u Engelstalige *boeken/kranten*?** fuhr·koapt ew ehng·uhls·taa·lih·khuh boo·kuhn/krahn·tuhn
I'd like…	**Ik wil graag...** ihk vihl khraakh…
– chewing gum	**– wat kauwgom** vaht kow·khohm
– cigars	**– wat sigaren** vaht see·khaa·ruhn
– a *pack/carton* of cigarettes	**– een *pakje/slof* sigaretten** uhn pahk·yuh/slohf see·khaa·reh·tuhn
– a lighter	**– een aansteker** uhn aan·stay·kuhr
– a magazine	**– een tijdschrift** uhn tiet·skhrihft
– matches	**– wat lucifers** vaht lew·see·fehrs

| – a *road/town* map of… | **– een *wegenkaart/stadsplattegrond* van…** uhn <u>vay</u>·khuhn·kaart/stahts·plah·tuh·<u>khrohnt</u> fahn… |
| – stamps | **– wat postzegels** vaht pohst·<u>zay</u>·khuhls |

Photography

I'm looking for… camera.	**Ik zoek…fototoestel.** ihk zook… <u>foa</u>·toa·<u>too</u>·stehl
– an automatic	**– een automatisch** uhn <u>oa</u>·toa·<u>maa</u>·tees
– a digital	**– een digitaal** uhn dee·khee·<u>taal</u>
– a disposable	**– een wegwerp** uhn <u>vehkh</u>·wehrp
I'd like…	**Ik wil graag…** ihk vihl khraakh…
– a battery	**– een batterij** uhn bah·tuh·<u>rle</u>
– digital prints	**– digitale afdrukken** dee·khee·<u>taa</u>·luh <u>ahf</u>·druh·kuhn
– a memory card	**– een geheugenkaart** uhn khuh·<u>hu</u>·khuhn·kaart
Can I print digital photos here?	**Kan ik hier digitale foto's afdrukken?** kahn ihk heer <u>dee</u>·khee·taa·luh <u>foa</u>·toas <u>ahf</u>·druh·kuhn

Sports and Leisure

Essential

When's the game?	**Wanneer is de wedstrijd?** <u>vah</u>·nayr ihs duh <u>veht</u>·striet
Where's…?	**Waar is…?** vaar ihs…
– the beach	**– het strand** heht strahnt
– the park	**– het park** heht pahrk
– the pool	**– het zwembad** heht <u>zvehm</u>·baht

Is it safe to *swim/dive* here?	**Is het veilig om hier te *zwemmen/duiken*?** ihs heht fie·lihkh ohm heer tuh *zveh·muhn/daw·kuhn*
Can I rent [hire] golf clubs?	**Kan ik golfclubs huren?** kahn ihk gohlf·kluhps hew·ruhn
What are the charges per hour?	**Hoeveel kost het per uur?** hoo·fayl kohst heht pehr ewr
How far is it to…?	**Hoe ver is het naar…?** hoo fehr ihs heht naar…
Can you show me on the map?	**Kunt u me dat op de kaart laten zien?** kuhnt ew muh daht ohp duh kaart laa·tuhn zeen

Spectator Sports

When's…? **Wanneer is…?** vah·nayr ihs…

– the basketball game
– **de basketbalwedstrijd** duh bahs·kuht·bahl·weht·striet

– the boxing match
– **de bokswedstrijd** duh bohks·weht·striet

– the cycling race
– **de wielerwedstrijd** duh vee·luhr·weht·striet

– the golf tournament
– **het golftoernooi** heht gohlf·toor·noay

– the soccer [football] game
– **de voetbalwedstrijd** duh foot·bahl·weht·striet

– the tennis match
– **de tennismatch** duh teh·nihs·mehtsh

– the volleyball game
– **de volleybalwedstrijd** duh voh·lee·bahl·weht·striet

Which teams are playing? **Welke teams spelen er?** vehl·kuh teems spay·luhn ehr

Where's…? **Waar is…?** vaar ihs…

– the horsetrack
– **de paardenrenbaan** duh paar·duhn·rehn·baan

| – the racetrack | **– het circuit** heht suhr·<u>kvee</u> |
| – the stadium | **– het stadion** heht <u>staa</u>·dee·yohn |

Cycling, both **fietsen** (leisure) and **wielrennen** (competitive), is very popular in the Netherlands. Other sports such as **voetbal** (soccer) and **hockey** (hockey) are also popular to watch and play. The Dutch are generally great fans of soccer and will wear the national color (orange) from head to toe while attending matches of the national soccer team.

Participating

Where *is/are...*?	**Waar *is/zijn...*?** vaar *Ihs/zien...*
– the golf course	**– de golfbaan** duh <u>gohlf</u>·baan
– the gym	**– de fitnessruimte** duh fiht·nuhs·<u>rawm</u>·tuh
– the park	**– het park** heht pahrk
– the tennis courts	**– de tennisbanen** duh <u>teh</u>·nihs·baa·nuhn

How much per...?	**Hoeveel kost het per...?** hoo·fayl kohst heht pehr...
– day	**– dag** dahkh
– hour	**– uur** ewr
– game	**– partij** pahr·<u>tie</u>
– round	**– ronde** <u>rohn</u>·duh
Can I rent [hire]...?	**Kan ik...huren?** kahn ihk...<u>hew</u>·ruhn
– golf clubs	**– golfclubs** <u>gohlf</u>·kluhps
– equipment	**– een uitrusting** uhn <u>awt</u>·ruhs·tihng
– a racket	**– een racket** uhn <u>rah</u>·kuht

At the Beach/Pool ——————————

Where's the *beach/ pool*?	**Waar is het *strand/zwembad*?** vaar ihs heht *strahnt/<u>zvehm</u>·baht*
Is there...?	**Is er...?** ihs ehr...
– a kiddie [paddling] pool	**– een kinderzwembad** uhn <u>kihn</u>·duhr·<u>zvehm</u>·baht
– an *indoor/outdoor* pool	**– een *binnenbad/buitenbad*** uhn <u>bih</u>·nuhn·baht/<u>baw</u>·tuhn·baht
– a lifeguard	**– een badmeester** uhn <u>baht</u>·mays·tuhr
Is it safe...?	**Is het veilig...?** ihs heht <u>fie</u>·lihkh...
– to swim	**– om te zwemmen** ohm tuh <u>zveh</u>·muhn
– to dive	**– om te duiken** ohm tuh <u>daw</u>·kuhn
– for children	**– voor kinderen** foar <u>kihn</u>·duh·ruhn
I want to rent [hire]...	**Ik wil...huren.** ihk vihl...<u>hew</u>·ruhn
– a deck chair	**– een ligstoel** uhn <u>lihkh</u>·stool
– a jet-ski	**– een jetski** uhn <u>dzheht</u>·skee

– a motorboat	– **een motorboot** uhn <u>moa</u>·tohr·boat
– a rowboat	– **een roeiboot** uhn <u>rooy</u>·boat
– a surfboard	– **een surfplank** uhn <u>suhrf</u>·plangk
– a towel	– **een handdoek** uhn <u>hahn</u>·dook
– an umbrella	– **een parasol** uhn <u>paa</u>·raa·sohl
– water skis	– **waterski's** <u>vaa</u>·tuhr·skees
– a windsurfer	– **een windsurfplank** uhn <u>vihnt</u>·suhrf·plahnk
For…hours.	**Voor…uur.** foar…ewr

▶ For travel with children, see page 139.

Zeilen (sailing) and other watersports are popular during the summer on **Friese meren** (the Frisian lakes) and in the more than 40 resorts along the coast. All different types of boats (including historic ships), canoes, windsurfers and water skis are available for rental. The Netherlands Board of Tourism publishes brochures with practical information and itineraries. Ask for information at the local tourist information office.

Winter Sports

A ticket for the skating rink, please.	**Een kaartje voor de ijsbaan, alstublieft.** uhn <u>kaart</u>·yuh foar duh <u>ies</u>·baan ahls·tew·<u>bleeft</u>
I want to rent [hire] ice skates.	**Ik wil schaatsen huren.** ihk vihl <u>skhaat</u>·suhn <u>hew</u>·ruhn
These are too *big/small*.	**Deze zijn te *groot/klein*.** <u>day</u>·zuh zien tuh *khroat/klien*
Can I take skating lessons?	**Kan ik schaatslessen nemen?** kahn ihk <u>skhaats</u>·leh·suhn <u>nay</u>·muhn

In the Countryside

I'd like a map of... **Ik wil graag een kaart van...** ihk vihl khraakh uhn kaart fahn...

– this region **– deze regio** <u>day</u>·zuh <u>ray</u>·khee·oa

– the walking routes **– de wandelroutes** duh <u>vahn</u>·duhl·<u>roo</u>·tuhs

– the bike routes **– de fietsroutes** duh <u>feets</u>·roo·tuhs

– the trails **– de wandelpaden** duh <u>vahn</u>·duhl·<u>paa</u>·duhn

Is it *easy/difficult*? **Is het *makkelijk/moeilijk?*** ihs heht <u>mah</u>·kuh·luhk/<u>mooy</u>·luhk

Is it *far/steep*? **Is het *ver/steil?*** ihs heht fehr/stiel

How far is it to...? **Hoe ver is het naar...?** hoo fehr ihs heht naar...

Can you show me on the map? **Kunt u me dat op de kaart laten zien?** kuhnt ew muh daht ohp duh <u>kaart laa</u>·tuhn zeen

I'm lost. **Ik ben verdwaald.** ihk behn fuhr·<u>dwaalt</u>

Where is...? **Waar is...?** vaar ihs...

– the bridge **– de brug** duh bruhkh

– the cave **– de grot** duh khroht

– the farm **– de boerderij** duh <u>boor</u>·duh·rie

– the forest **– het bos** heht bohs

– the lake **– het meer** heht mayr

– the nature preserve **– het natuurreservaat** heht naa·<u>tewr</u>·ray·zuhr·<u>faat</u>

– the overlook **– het uitkijkpunt** heht <u>awt</u>·kiek·puhnt

– the park **– het park** heht pahrk

– the path **– het pad** het paht

– the picnic area **– het picknickgebied** heht <u>pihk</u>·nihk·khuh·beet

– the river **– de rivier** duh ree·<u>feer</u>

– the sea **– de zee** duh zay

Culture and Nightlife

Essential

What is there to do in the evenings?	**Wat is er 's avonds te doen?** vaht ihs ehr <u>saa</u>·vohnts tuh doon
Do you have a program of events?	**Heeft u een evenementenprogramma?** hayft ew uhn ay·fuh·nuh·<u>mehn</u>·tuhn·<u>proa</u>·khrah·maa
What's playing at the movies [cinema] tonight?	**Welke films draaien er vanavond?** <u>vehl</u>·kuh fihlms <u>draa</u>·yuhn ehr fah·<u>naa</u>·fohnt
Where's...?	**Waar is...?** vaar ihs...
– the downtown area	– **het stadscentrum** heht <u>staht</u>·sehn·truhm
– the bar	– **de bar** duh bahr
– the dance club	– **de discotheek** duh dihs·koa·<u>tayk</u>
Is there a cover charge?	**Moet ik entree betalen?** moot ihk ahn·<u>tray</u> buh·<u>taa</u>·luhn

> The Netherlands has a strong tradition in the arts. There are hundreds of museums to be explored, many featuring work by famous Dutch artists such as Rembrandt, Van Gogh and Vermeer, to name a few. Price of admission varies, though some are free.
>
> Amsterdam is home to the national opera, ballet and theater companies, while The Hague and Rotterdam each have their own resident orchestras and dance companies. Cultural, musical and theater events are scheduled throughout the year; check with the tourist information office to see what's going on while you're in town.

Entertainment

Can you recommend...?	**Kunt u...aanbevelen?** kuhnt ew... <u>aan</u>·buh·fay·luhn
– a concert	**– een concert** <u>uhn</u> kohn·<u>sehrt</u>
– a movie [film]	**– een film** uhn film
– an opera	**– een opera** uhn <u>oa</u>·puh·raa
– a play	**– een toneelstuk** uhn toa·<u>nayl</u>·stuhk
When does it *start/ end*?	**Wanneer *begint/eindigt* het?** <u>vah</u>·nayr buh·<u>khihnt/ien</u>·dihkht heht
What's the dress code?	**Zijn er kledingvoorschriften?** zien ehr <u>klay</u>·dihng·<u>foar</u>·skrihf·tuhn
I really like...	**Ik hou erg van...** ihk how ehrkh fahn...
– classical music	**– klassieke muziek** klah·<u>see</u>·kuh mew·<u>zeek</u>
– folk music	**– volksmuziek** <u>fohlks</u>·mew·zeek
– jazz	**– jazz** jehz
– pop music	**– popmuziek** <u>pohp</u>·mew·zeek
– rap	**– rap** rehp

▶ For ticketing, see page 19.

There are a number of festivals scheduled throughout the year in the Netherlands, some with moveable dates. The local tourist information office, hotels and guidebooks offer extensive information about local as well as national celebrations.

The biggest Dutch celebration every year across the country by far is **Koninginnedag** (Queen's Day). Celebrated on April 30th, when the weather in the Netherlands is mild, this giant open-air party features concerts and events, including the **vrijmarkt** (freemarket). **Koninginnedag** is the one day of the year when anyone is allowed to sell anything tax-free.

You May Hear...

Zet uw mobiele telefoon uit.
zeht ew moa·<u>bee</u>·luh tay·luh·<u>foan</u> awt

Turn off your cell [mobile] phones.

Nightlife

What is there to do in the evenings?	**Wat is er 's avonds te doen?** vaht ihs ehr <u>saa</u>·vohnts tuh doon
Can you recommend...?	**Kunt u...aanbevelen?** kuhnt ew... <u>aan</u>·buh·fay·luhn
– a bar	**– een bar** uhn bahr
– a casino	**– een casino** uhn kaa·<u>see</u>·noa
– a dance club	**– een discotheek** uhn dihs·koa·<u>tayk</u>
– a gay club	**– een homoclub** uhn <u>hoa</u>·moa·club
– a nightclub	**– een nachtclub** uhn <u>nahkht</u>·kluhp
Is there live music?	**Is er livemuziek?** ihs ehr laaif·mew·<u>zeek</u>
How do I get there?	**Hoe kom ik er?** hoo kohm ihk ehr
Is there an admission charge?	**Moet ik entree betalen?** moot ihk ahn·<u>tray</u> buh·<u>taa</u>·luhn
Let's go dancing.	**Laten we gaan dansen.** <u>laa</u>·tuhn vuh khaan <u>dahn</u>·suhn

After dark, the Netherlands has a lot to offer depending on what you're in the mood for. In Amsterdam, the action is centered in three main areas. If you're looking for dance and night clubs, head to Leidseplein. For clubs, cabarets and strip shows, go to Rembrandtplein. The Red Light District is world-famous for offering a range of alternative activities.

For a low key evening, check out a "brown" cafe (traditional Dutch bar), pub or bar. Amsterdam is home to about a thousand, so you can easily find one that fits your style.

▼ Special Needs

Essential

I'm here on business.	**Ik ben hier voor zaken.** ihk behn heer foar <u>zaa</u>·kuhn
Here's my business card.	**Hier is mijn visitekaartje.** heer ihs mien fee·<u>zee</u>·tuh·kaart·yuh
Can I have your card?	**Mag ik uw visitekaartje?** mahkh ihk ew fee·<u>zee</u>·tuh·kaart·yuh
I have a meeting with...	**Ik heb een afspraak met...** ihk hehp uhn <u>ahf</u>·spraak meht...
Where's...?	**Waar is...?** vaar ihs...
– the business center	**– het bedrijvencomplex** heht buh·<u>drie</u>·fuhn·kohm·plehks
– the convention hall	**– het congresgebouw** heht kohn·<u>khrehs</u>·khuh·bow
– the meeting room	**– de vergaderruimte** duh fuhr·<u>khaa</u>·duhr·rawm·tuh

Business Communication ————

I'm here to attend...	**Ik ben hier voor...** ihk behn heer foar...
– a seminar	**– een seminar** uhn <u>seh</u>·mee·nahr
– a conference	**– een conferentie** uhn kohn·fuh·<u>rehnt</u>·see
– a meeting	**– een vergadering** uhn fuhr·<u>khaa</u>·duh·rihng
My name is...	**Mijn naam is...** mien naam ihs...
May I introduce my colleague...?	**Mag ik mijn collega...voorstellen?** mahkh ihk mien koh·<u>lay</u>·kha...<u>foar</u>·steh·luhn
I'm sorry I'm late.	**Sorry dat ik te laat ben.** <u>soh</u>·ree daht ihk tuh laat behn
I'd like an interpreter.	**Ik wil graag een tolk.** ihk vihl khraag uhn tohlk

You can reach me at the...Hotel,	**U kunt me in hotel...bereiken.** ew kuhnt muh ihn hoh·<u>tehl</u>...buh·<u>rie</u>·kuhn
I'm here until...	**Ik ben hier tot...** ihk behn heer toht...
I need to...	**Ik wil...** ihk vihl...
– make a call	**– bellen** <u>beh</u>·luhn
– make a photocopy	**– iets kopiëren** eets <u>koa</u>·pee·yay·ruhn
– send an e-mail	**– een e-mail sturen** uhn <u>ee</u>·mayl <u>stew</u>·ruhn
– send a fax	**– een fax sturen** uhn fahks <u>stew</u>·ruhn
– send a package (overnight)	**– een pakketje (overnight) versturen** uhn pah·<u>keht</u>·yuh (oa·fuhr·<u>niet</u>) fuhr·<u>stew</u>·ruhn
It was a pleasure to meet you.	**Het was aangenaam om kennis met u te maken.** heht wahs <u>aan</u>·khuh·naam ohm <u>keh</u>·nihs meht ew tuh <u>maa</u>·kuhn

▶For internet and communications, see page 45.

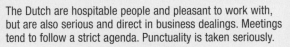 The Dutch are hospitable people and pleasant to work with, but are also serious and direct in business dealings. Meetings tend to follow a strict agenda. Punctuality is taken seriously.

You May Hear...

Heeft u een afspraak? hayft ew uhn ahf·spraak Do you have an appointment?

Met wie? meht vee With whom?

Hij♂/Zij♀ is in een vergadering. hie♂/zie♀ ihs ihn uhn fuhr·khaa·duh·rihng He/She is in a meeting.

Een ogenblik, alstublieft. uhn oa·khuhn·blihk ahls·tew·bleeft One moment, please.

Bedankt voor uw komst. buh·dangkt foar ew kohmst Thank you for coming.

Travel with Children

Essential

Is there a discount for children? | **Is er korting voor kinderen?** ihs ehr kohr·tihng foar kihn·duh·ruhn

Can you recommend a babysitter? | **Kunt u een oppas aanbevelen?** kuhnt ew uhn ohp·pahs aan·buh·fay·luhn

Can I have a highchair? | **Mogen we een kinderstoel?** moa·khuhn vuh uhn kihn·duhr·stool

Where can I change the baby? | **Waar kan ik de baby verschonen?** vaar kahn ihk duh bay·bee fuhr·skhoa·nuhn

Fun with Kids

Can you recommend something for the kids? | **Kunt u iets aanbevelen voor de kinderen?** kuhnt ew eets aan·buh·fay·luhn foar duh kihn·duh·ruhn

Where's...? | **Waar is...?** vaar ihs...

– the amusement park | **– het pretpark** heht preht·pahrk

Where's...?	**Waar is...?** vaar ihs...
– the arcade	**– de speelhal** duh <u>spayl</u>·hahl
– the kiddie [paddling] pool	**– het kinderzwembad** heht <u>kihn</u>·duhr·zvehm·baht
– the park	**– het park** heht pahrk
– the playground	**– de speeltuin** duh <u>spayl</u>·tawn
– the zoo	**– de dierentuin** duh <u>dee</u>·ruhn·tawn
Are kids allowed?	**Zijn kinderen daar toegestaan?** zien <u>kihn</u>·duh·ruhn daar <u>too</u>·khuh·staan
Is it safe for kids?	**Is het veilig voor kinderen?** ihs heht <u>fie</u>·lihkh foar <u>kihn</u>·duh·ruhn
Is it suitable for... year-olds?	**Is het geschikt voor kinderen van... jaar?** ihs heht khuh·<u>skhihkt</u> foar <u>kihn</u>·duh·ruhn fahn...yaar

▶ For numbers, see page 158.

You May Hear...

Wat schattig! vaht <u>skhah</u>·tihkh	How cute!
Hoe heet hij♂/zij♀? hoo hayt hie♂/zie♀	What's his/her name?
Hoe oud is hij♂/zij♀? hoo owt ihs hie♂/zie♀	How old is he/she?

Basic Needs for Kids

Do you have...?	**Heeft u...?** hayft ew...
– a baby bottle	**– een babyfles** uhn <u>bay</u>·bee·flehs
– baby wipes	**– babydoekjes** <u>bay</u>·bee·<u>dook</u>·yuhs
– a car seat	**– een kinderzitje** uhn <u>kihn</u>·duhr·ziht·yuh
– a children's menu/portion	**– een *kindermenu/kinderportie*** uhn <u>kihn</u>·duhr·muh·<u>new</u>/kihn·duhr·<u>pohr</u>·see
– a highchair	**– een kinderstoel** uhn <u>kihn</u>·duhr·stool

– a crib/cot	**– een *wieg/kinderbedje*** uhn veekh/<u>kihn</u>·duhr·<u>beht</u>·yuh
– diapers [nappies]	**– luiers** <u>law</u>·yuhrs
– formula	**– flesvoeding** <u>flehs</u>·foo·dihng
– a pacifier [soother]	**– een fopspeen** uhn <u>fohp</u>·spayn
– a playpen	**– een babybox** uhn <u>bay</u>·bee·bohks
– a stroller [pushchair]	**– een kinderwagen** uhn <u>kihn</u>·duhr·vaa·khun
Can I breastfeed the baby here?	**Mag ik mijn baby hier de borst geven?** mahkh Ihk mien <u>bay</u>·bee heer duh bohrst <u>khay</u>·fuhn
Where can I change the baby?	**Waar kan ik de baby verschonen?** vaar kahn ihk duh <u>bay</u>·bee fuhr·<u>skhoa</u>·nuhn

▶ For dining with kids, see page 59.

Babysitting

| Can you recommend a babysitter? | **Kunt u een oppas aanbevelen?** kuhnt ew uhn <u>ohp</u>·pahs <u>aan</u>·buh·fay·luhn |
| What's the charge? | **Hoeveel kost het?** <u>hoo</u>·fayl kohst heht |

| We'll be back by… | **We zijn om…uur terug.** vuh zien ohm…ewr truhkh |

▶ For time, see page 160.

| I can be reached at… | **U kunt me bij…bereiken.** ew kuhnt muh bie…buh·<u>rie</u>·kuhn |

Health and Emergency ─────────────

Can you recommend a pediatrician?	**Kunt u een kinderarts aanbevelen?** kuhnt ew uhn <u>kihn</u>·duhr·ahrts <u>aan</u>·buh·fay·luhn
My child is allergic to…	**Mijn kind is allergisch voor…** mien kihnt ihs ah·<u>lehr</u>·khees foar…
My child is missing.	**Ik ben mijn kind kwijt.** ihk behn mien kihnt kviet
Have you seen a *boy/girl*?	**Heeft u een *jongen/meisje* gezien?** hayft ew uhn *<u>yohng</u>·uhn/<u>mies</u>·yuh* khuh·<u>zeen</u>

▶ For food items, see page 75.
▶ For health, see page 147.
▶ For police, see page 145.

For the Disabled

Essential

Is there access for the disabled?	**Is het toegankelijk voor gehandicapten?** is heht too·<u>khahng</u>·kuh·luhk foar khuh·<u>hehn</u>·dee·kehp·tuhn
Is there a wheelchair ramp?	**Is er een rolstoeloprit?** uhn <u>rohl</u>·stool·<u>ohp</u>·riht
Is there a handicapped- [disabled-] accessible toilet?	**Is er een toilet dat toegankelijk is voor gehandicapten?** uhn tvaa·<u>leht</u> daht too·<u>khahng</u>·kuh·luhk ihs foar khuh·<u>hehn</u>·dee·kehp·tuhn

I need...	**Ik heb...nodig.** ihk hehp..._noa_·dihkh
– assistance	**– hulp** huhlp
– an elevator [lift]	**– een lift** uhn lihft
– a ground-floor room	**– een kamer op de begane grond** uhn _kaa_·muhr ohp duh buh·_khaa_·nuh khrohnt

Getting Help

I'm disabled.	**Ik ben gehandicapt.** ihk behn khuh·_hehn_·dee·kehpt
I'm deaf.	**Ik ben doof.** ihk behn doaf
I'm *visually/hearing* impaired.	**Ik ben *slechtziend/slechthorend.*** ihk behn *slehkht·_zeent_/slehkht·_hoa_·ruhnt*
I'm unable to *walk far/use the stairs.*	**Ik kan niet *ver lopen/de trap gebruiken.*** ihk kahn neet *fehr _loa_·puhn/duh trahp khuh·_braw_·kuhn*
Can I bring my wheelchair?	**Kan ik mijn rolstoel meenemen?** kahn ihk mien _rohl_·stool _may_·nay·muhn
Are guide dogs permitted?	**Zijn geleidehonden toegestaan?** zien khuh·_lei_·duh·_hohn_·duhn _too_·khuh·staan
Can you help me?	**Kunt u me helpen?** kuhnt ew muh _hehl_·puhn
Can you *open/hold* the door?	**Kunt u de deur *openen/openhouden?*** kuhnt ew duh dur _oa_·puh·nuhn/_oa_·puhn _how_·duhn

▼ Resources

Emergencies

Essential

Help!	**Help!** hehlp
Go away!	**Ga weg!** khaa vehkh
Stop thief!	**Houd de dief!** howt duh deef
Get a doctor!	**Haal een dokter!** haal uhn <u>dohk</u>·tuhr
Fire!	**Brand!** brahnt
I'm lost.	**Ik ben verdwaald.** ihk behn fuhr·<u>dvaalt</u>
Can you help me?	**Kunt u me helpen?** kuhnt ew muh <u>hehl</u>·puhn

Police

Essential

Call the police!	**Bel de politie!** bel duh poa·<u>leet</u>·see
Where's the police station?	**Waar is het politiebureau?** vaar ihs heht poa·<u>leet</u>·see·bew·roa
There's been an accident.	**Er heeft een ongeluk plaatsgevonden.** ehr hayft uhn <u>ohn</u>·khuh·luhk plaats·khuh·<u>fohn</u>·duhn
My child is missing.	**Ik ben mijn kind kwijt.** ihk behn mien kihnt kviet
I need...	**Ik wil...** ihk vihl...
– an interpreter	– **gebruikmaken van een tolk** khuh·<u>brawk</u> <u>maa</u>·kuhn fahn uhn tohlk
– to contact my lawyer	– **mijn advocaat spreken** mien at·foa·<u>kaat</u> <u>spray</u>·kuhn
– to make a phone call	– **iemand bellen** <u>ee</u>·mahnt <u>beh</u>·luhn
I'm innocent.	**Ik ben onschuldig.** ihk behn ohn·<u>skhuhl</u>·dihkh

145

You May Hear...

Mag ik uw legitimatiebewijs zien? mahkh ihk ew lay·khee·tee·maat·see zeen

Can I see your identification?

Wanneer/Waar is het gebeurd? vah·nayr/vaar ihs heht khuh·burt

When/Where did it happen?

Hoe ziet hij♂/zij♀ eruit? hoo zeet hie♂/zie♀ ehr·awt

What does he/she look like?

▶For emergency numbers, see page 51.

Lost Property and Theft

I want to report...	**Ik wil...melden.** ihk vihl...<u>mehl</u>·duhn	
– a mugging	**– een beroving** uhn buh·<u>roa</u>·fihng	
– a rape	**– een verkrachting** uhn fuhr·<u>krahkh</u>·tihng	
– a theft	**– een diefstal** uhn <u>deef</u>·stahl	

I've been *robbed/ mugged*. **Ik ben *beroofd/overvallen.*** ihk behn buh·<u>roaft</u>/<u>oa</u>·fuhr·<u>fah</u>·luhn

I've lost my... **Ik heb mijn...verloren.** ihk hehp mien... fuhr·<u>loa</u>·ruhn

My...*was/were* stolen. **Mijn...*is/zijn* gestolen.** mien...ihs/zien khuh·<u>stoa</u>·luhn

– backpack	**– rugzak** <u>ruhkh</u>·zahk	
– bicycle	**– fiets** feets	
– camera	**– fototoestel** <u>foa</u>·toa·<u>too</u>·stehl	
– car/rental car	**– auto/huurauto** <u>ow</u>·toa/<u>hewr</u>·<u>ow</u>·toa	
– computer	**– computer** kohm·<u>pyoo</u>·tuhr	
– credit card	**– creditcard** <u>kreh</u>·diht·kaart	
– jewelry	**– sieraden** <u>see</u>·raa·duhn	
– money	**– geld** khehlt	

– purse [handbag]	**– handtas** hahn·tahs
– traveler's checks [cheques]	**– reischeques** ries·shehks
– wallet	**– portemonnee** pohr·tuh·moh·nay

Health

Essential

I'm sick [ill].	**Ik ben ziek.** ihk behn zeek
I need an English-speaking doctor.	**Ik zoek een dokter die Engels spreekt.** ihk zook uhn dohk·tuhr dee ehng·uhls spraykt
It hurts here.	**Het doet hier pijn.** heht doot heer pien
I have a stomachache.	**Ik heb maagpijn.** ihk hehp maakh·pien

Finding a Doctor

Can you recommend a *doctor/dentist*?	**Kunt u een *dokter/tandarts* aanbevelen?** kuhnt ew uhn *dohk·tuhr/ tahnt·ahrts* aan·buh·fay·luhn
Can the doctor come to see me here?	**Kan de dokter naar mij toekomen?** kahn duh dohk·tuhr naar mie too·koa·muhn
What are the office hours?	**Wat zijn de openingstijden?** vaht zien duh oa·puh·nihngs·tie·duhn
Can I make an appointment for *today/tomorrow*?	**Kan ik een afspraak maken voor *vandaag/morgen*?** kahn ihk uhn ahf·spraak maa·kuhn foar *fahn·daakh/mohr·khuhn*
It's urgent.	**Het is dringend.** heht ihs drihng·uhnt

Symptoms

I'm…	**Ik…** ihk…
– bleeding	– **bloed** bloot
– constipated	– **heb last van constipatie** hehp lahst fahn kohn·stee·paat·see
– dizzy	– **ben duizelig** behn daw·zuh·luhkh
– nauseous	– **ben misselijk** behn mih·suh·luhk
– vomiting	– **moet overgeven** moot oa·fuhr·khay·fuhn
It hurts here.	**Het doet hier pijn.** heht doot heer pien
I have…	**Ik heb…** ihk hehp…
– an allergic reaction	– **een allergische reactie** uhn ah·lehr·khee·suh ray·ahk·see
– chest pain	– **pijn op mijn borst** pien ohp mien bohrst
– an earache	– **oorpijn** oar·pien
– a fever	– **koorts** koarts
– pain	– **pijn** pien
– a rash	– **huiduitslag** hawt·awt·slahkh
– a sprain	– **iets verstuikt** eets fuhr·stawkt
– a stomachache	– **maagpijn** maakh·pien
I have some swelling.	**Het is opgezet.** heht ihs ohp·khuh·zeht
I've been sick [ill] for…days.	**Ik ben al…dagen ziek.** ihk behn ahl… daa·khuhn zeek

▶For numbers, see page 158.

Health Conditions

I'm anemic.	**Ik heb bloedarmoede.** ihk hehp <u>bloot</u>·ahr·<u>moo</u>·duh
I'm diabetic.	**Ik ben suikerpatiënt.** ihk behn <u>saw</u>·kuhr·paa·<u>shehnt</u>
I have asthma.	**Ik heb astma.** ihk hehp <u>ahs</u>·maa
I'm allergic to *antibiotics/penicillin.*	**Ik ben allergisch voor *antibiotica/ penicilline.*** ihk behn ah·<u>lehr</u>·khees foar *ahn·tee·bee·<u>oa</u>·tee·kaa/<u>pay</u>·nee·see·<u>lee</u>·nuh*

▶ For food items, see page 75.

I have…	**Ik heb…** ihk hehp…
– arthritis	**– artritis** ahrt·<u>ree</u>·tihs
– *high/low* blood pressure	**– *hoge/lage* bloeddruk** <u>hoa</u>·khuh/<u>laa</u>·khuh <u>bloot</u>·druhk
– a heart condition	**– een hartkwaal** uhn <u>hahrt</u>·kvaal
I'm on…	**Ik neem…** ihk naym…

You May Hear…

Wat is er mis? vaht ihs ehr mihs	What's wrong?
Waar doet het pijn? vaar doot heht pien	Where does it hurt?
Neemt u andere medicijnen? naymt ew ahn·duh·ruh may·dee·<u>sie</u>·nuhn	Are you taking any other medication?
Bent u ergens allergisch voor? behtn ew <u>ehr</u>·khuhns ah·<u>lehr</u>·khees foar	Are you allergic to anything?
Kunt u uw mond openen? kuhnt ew eww mohnt <u>oa</u>·puh·nuhn	Open your mouth.
Even diep ademhalen. <u>ay</u>·fuhn deep <u>aa</u>·duhm·<u>haa</u>·luhn	Breathe deeply.

Hospital

| Can you notify my family? | **Kunt u mijn familie op de hoogte brengen?** kuhnt ew mien faa·<u>mee</u>·lee ohp duh <u>hoakh</u>·tuh <u>brehng</u>·uhn |
| Can you notify my family? | |

Can you notify my family?
Kunt u mijn familie op de hoogte brengen? kuhnt ew mien faa·<u>mee</u>·lee ohp duh <u>hoakh</u>·tuh <u>brehng</u>·uhn

I'm in pain.
Ik heb pijn. ik hehp pien

I need a *doctor/nurse*.
Ik heb een *dokter/verpleegster* nodig. ihk hehp uhn *<u>dohk</u>·tuhr/fuhr·<u>playkh</u>·stuhr* <u>noa</u>·dihkh

When are visiting hours?
Wanneer is het bezoekuur? <u>vah</u>·nayr ihs heht buh·<u>zook</u>·ewr

I'm visiting…
Ik kom op bezoek bij… ihk kohm ohp buh·<u>zook</u> bie…

Dentist

I've *broken a tooth/ lost a filling*.
Ik *heb een tand gebroken/ben een vulling verloren*. ihk *hehp uhn tahnt khuh·<u>broa</u>·kuhn/ behn uhn <u>fuh</u>·lihng fuhr·<u>loa</u>·ruhn*

I have toothache.
Ik heb kiespijn. ihk hehp <u>kees</u>·pien

Can you fix this denture?
Kunt u dit kunstgebit repareren? kuhnt ew diht <u>kuhnst</u>·khuh·biht ray·paa·<u>ray</u>·ruhn

Gynecologist

I have *menstrual cramps/a vaginal infection*.
Ik heb *menstruatiepijn/een vaginale infectie*. ihk hehp *mehn·strew·<u>aat</u>·see·pien/uhn faa·khih·<u>naa</u>·luh ihn·<u>fehk</u>·see*

I missed my period.
Ik ben niet ongesteld geworden. ihk behn neet ohn·khuh·<u>stehlt</u> khuh·<u>vohr</u>·duhn

I'm on the Pill.
Ik ben aan de pil. ihk behn aan duh pihl

I'm (not) pregnant.
Ik ben (niet) zwanger. ihk behn (neet) <u>zvahng</u>·uhr

| I haven't had my period for…months. | **Ik ben al…maanden niet ongesteld geweest.** ihk behn ahl…<u>maan</u>·duh neet ohn·khuh·<u>stehlt</u> khuh·<u>vayst</u> |

▶For numbers, see page 158.

Optician

I've lost…	**Ik heb…verloren.** ihk hehp…fuhr·<u>loa</u>·ruhn
– a contact lens	**– een van mijn contactlenzen** ayn fahn mien kohn·<u>tahkt</u>·lehn·zuhn
– my glasses	**– mijn bril** mien brlhl
– a lens	**– een lens** uhn lehns

Payment and Insurance

How much?	**Hoeveel kost het?** <u>hoo</u>·fayl kohst heht
Can I pay by credit card?	**Kan ik met een creditcard betalen?** kahn ihk meht uhn <u>khreh</u>·diht·kaart buh·<u>taa</u>·luhn
I have insurance.	**Ik ben verzekerd.** ihk behn fuhr·<u>zay</u>·kuhrt
Can I have a receipt for my insurance?	**Mag ik een kwitantie hebben voor mijn verzekering?** mahkh ihk uhn kvee·<u>tahnt</u>·see <u>heh</u>·buhn foar mien fuhr·<u>zay</u>·kuh·rihng

151

Pharmacy [Chemist]

Essential

Where's the nearest pharmacy [chemist]?	**Waar is de dichtstbijzijnde apotheek?** vaar ihs duh <u>dihkhtst</u>·bie·<u>zien</u>·duh ah·poa·<u>tayk</u>
What time does the pharmacy [chemist] *open/close*?	**Hoe laat gaat de apotheek *open/dicht*?** hoo laat khaat duh ah·poa·<u>tayk</u> <u>oa</u>·puhn/dihkht
What would you recommend for…?	**Wat zou u aanbevelen voor…?** vaht zow ew <u>aan</u>·buh·<u>fay</u>·luhn foar…
How much should I take?	**Hoeveel moet ik er innemen?** <u>hoo</u>·fayl moot ihk ehr <u>ihn</u>·nay·muhn
Can you fill [make up] this prescription for me?	**Kunt u dit recept voor me klaarmaken?** kuhnt ew diht ruh·<u>sehpt</u> foar muh <u>klaar</u>·maa·kuhn
I'm allergic to…	**Ik ben allergisch voor…** ihk behn ah·<u>lehr</u>·khees foar…

The **apotheek** (pharmacy) fills medical prescriptions and the **drogisterij** (drug store) sells non-prescription items, toiletries and cosmetics. Regular hours are Monday to Friday from 8 or 9 a.m. to around 6 p.m. On nights and weekends, pharmacies open on a rotating schedule. Check the sign on a pharmacy window to find the closest open pharmacy.

Dosage Instructions

How much should I take?	**Hoeveel moet ik er innemen?** <u>hoo</u>·fayl moot ihk ehr <u>ihn</u>·nay·muhn
How often?	**Hoe vaak per dag?** hoo·faak pehr dahkh
Is it suitable for children?	**Is het geschikt voor kinderen?** ihs heht khuh·<u>skhihkt</u> foar <u>kihn</u>·duh·ruhn

I'm taking…	**Ik neem…** ihk naym…
Are there side effects?	**Zijn er bijwerkingen?** zien ehr <u>bie</u>·vehr·kihng·uhn

You May See…

EEN/DRIE KEER PER DAG	once/three times a day
TABLETTEN	tablets
DRUPPEL	drop
VOOR/NA/BIJ MAALTIJDEN	before/after/with meals
OP EEN LEGE MAAG	on an empty stomach

Health Problems

I'd like some medicine for…	**Ik wil graag medicijnen tegen…** ihk vihl khraakh may·dee·<u>sie</u>·nuhn <u>tay</u>·khuhn…
– a cold	**– verkoudheid** fuhr·<u>kowt</u>·hiet
– a cough	**– hoesten** <u>hoos</u>·tuhn
– diarrhea	**– diarree** dee·ah·<u>ray</u>
– motion [travel] sickness	**– reisziekte** <u>ries</u>·zeek·tuh
– a sore throat	**– keelpijn** <u>kayl</u>·pien
– sunburn	**– zonnebrand** <u>zoh</u>·nuh·branht
– an upset stomach	**– maagpijn** <u>maakh</u>·pien

Basic Needs

I'd like…	**Ik wil graag…** ihk vihl khraakh…
– acetaminophen [paracetamol]	**– paracetamol** <u>paa</u>·raa·say·taa·<u>mohl</u>
– antiseptic cream	**– antiseptische crème** <u>ahn</u>·tee·<u>sehp</u>·tee·suh <u>kreh</u>·muh

I'd like…	**Ik wil graag…** ihk vihl khraakh…
– aspirin	**– aspirine** ahs·pee·ree·nuh
– bandages [plasters]	**– pleisters** plies·tuhrs
– a comb	**– een kam** uhn kahm
– condoms	**– condooms** kohn·doams
– contact lens solution	**– contactlensvloeistof** kohn·tahkt·lehns·flooy·stohf
– deodorant	**– deodorant** day·oa·doa·rahnt
– hair spray	**– haarspray** haar·spray
– ibuprofen	**– ibuprofen** ee·bew·proa·fehn
– insect repellent	**– insektenspray** ihn·sehk·tuhn·spray
– a nail file	**– een nagelvijl** uhn naa·khuhl·fiel
– (disposable) razors	**– wegwerpscheermesjes** vehkh·vehrp·skhayr·mehs·yuhs
– razor blades	**– scheermesjes** skhayr·mehs·yuhs
– sanitary napkins [pads]	**– maandverband** maant·fuhr·bahnt
– shampoo/ conditioner	**– shampoo/conditioner** shahm·poa/kohn·dih·shuh·nuhr
– soap	**– zeep** zayp
– sunscreen	**– zonnebrandcrème** zoh·nuh·brahnt·kreh·muh
– tampons	**– tampons** tahm·pohns
– tissues	**– tissues** tih·shoos
– toilet paper	**– toiletpapier** tvaa·leht·paa·peer
– a toothbrush	**– een tandenborstel** uhn tahn·duhn·bohr·stuhl
– toothpaste	**– tandpasta** tahnt·pahs·taa

▶ For baby products, see page 140.

Reference

Grammar

Regular Verbs

All regular Dutch verbs follow the same conjugation pattern in the present tense: add **-t** to the verb root in the second and third person singular (unless the verb ends in **t**), and add **-en** to the verb root in all plural forms. The past tense of regular verbs is formed by adding **-te(n)** or **-de(n)** to the root. The future tense consists of the auxiliary verb **zullen** (will) + infinitive. Below are the present, past and future forms of the regular verb **werken** (to work).

WERKEN (to work)		Present	Past	Future
I	**ik**	**werkt**	**werkte**	**zal werken**
you (sing., for./Inf.)	**u/jij**	**werkt**	**werkte**	**zal werken**
he/she	**hij/zij**	**werkt**	**werkte**	**zal werken**
we	**wij**	**werken**	**werkten**	**zullen werken**
you (pl.)	**jullie**	**werken**	**werkten**	**zullen werken**
they	**zij**	**werken**	**werkten**	**zullen werken**

Irregular Verbs

There are numerous irregular verbs in Dutch. These must be memorized. Below are the present tense conjugations for the frequently used verbs **hebben** (to have) and **zijn** (to be).

		HEBBEN (to have)	ZIJN (to be)
I	**ik**	**heb**	**ben**
you (sing., for./inf.)	**u/jij**	**heeft/hebt**	**bent**

for. = formal inf. = informal pl. = plural sing. = singular

		HEBBEN (to have)	**ZIJN** (to be)
he/she	**hij/zij**	**heeft**	**is**
we	**wij**	**hebben**	**zijn**
you (pl.)	**jullie**	**hebben**	**zijn**
they	**zij**	**hebben**	**zijn**

Nouns and Articles

Nouns are either masculine ♂, feminine ♀, or neuter. Masculine and feminine nouns take the definite article **de**, neuter nouns take **het**. All nouns take the indefinite article **een** (a/an).

The plural is generally formed by adding **en**; most nouns ending with **je**, **el**, **em**, **en** and **aar** take **s**. For few nouns, the plural is formed by adding **'s**:

de deur (the door), **de deuren** (the doors)

het huis (the house), **de huizen** (the houses)

het café (the cafe), **de cafés** (the cafes)

de bikini (the bikini), **de bikini's** (the bikini's)

Word Order

Word order in Dutch is generally as in English, i.e. subject-verb-object.

De man zoekt de fiets. The man searches for the bike.

Questions can be formed in Dutch:

1. by inverting the subject and verb:

Kunt u me helpen?   Can you help me?

2. by using a question word + the inverted order:

Waar ben je?   Where are you?

Negation

To negate a statement, place **niet** (not) after the verb, or after the object.

Ik rook niet.   I don't smoke.

Ik heb de kaartjes niet.   I don't have the tickets.

For nouns, the negation is made by adding **geen**.

Ik heb geen sigaretten.   I have no cigarettes.

Imperatives

In Dutch, the imperative is derived from the second person plural or singluar (you) form in the present tense. When using the imperative with we, add **laten** (let) + the Infinitive, as in English.

you (inf.)	**Ga! (Go!)**
you (pl., inf.)	**Ga! (Go!)**
you (for.)	**Gaat! (Go!)**
we	**Laten we gaan! (Let's go!)**

Comparative and Superlative

In Dutch the comparative of an adjective is usually formed by adding **-er** to the end of the adjective. Examples:

klein (small)   **kleiner** (smaller)

The superlative of an adjective is usually formed by adding **-st** to the end of the adjective. Examples:

klein (small)   **kleinst** (smallest)

Adjectives

Adjectives usually end with an **e** (with the exception of a singular neuter noun), for example:

de kleine jongen (the small boy)

However, **e** is not added when the adjective follows the noun, or when the noun is preceded by **elk/ieder** (each), **veel** (much), **zulk** (such) and **geen** (no). Examples:

de jongen is klein (the boy is small)

geen warm water (no warm water)

Adverbs and Adverbial Expressions

In Dutch, adverbs are usually identical to the adjectives but, unlike adjectives, their endings don't change. Examples:

| Adjective: | **het lekkere eten** | the good food |
| Adverb: | **het eten is lekker** | the food is good |

Numbers

Essential	
0	**nul** nuhl
1	**één** ayn
2	**twee** tvay
3	**drie** dree
4	**vier** feer
5	**vijf** fief
6	**zes** zehs
7	**zeven** zay·fuhn
8	**acht** ahkht
9	**negen** nay·khuhn
10	**tien** teen
11	**elf** ehlf
12	**twaalf** tvaalf
13	**dertien** dehr·teen

14	**veertien** <u>fayr</u>·teen
15	**vijftien** <u>fief</u>·teen
16	**zestien** <u>zehs</u>·teen
17	**zeventien** <u>zay</u>·fuhn·teen
18	**achttien** <u>ahkh</u>·teen
19	**negentien** <u>nay</u>·khuhn·teen
20	**twintig** <u>tvihn</u>·tuhkh
21	**eenentwintig** <u>ayn</u>·uhn·tvihn·tuhkh
22	**tweeëntwintig** <u>tvay</u>·uhn·tvihn·tuhkh
30	**dertig** <u>dehr</u>·tihkh
31	**eenendertig** <u>ayn</u>·uhn·dehr·tihkh
40	**veertig** <u>fayr</u>·tihkh
50	**vijftig** <u>fief</u>·tihkh
60	**zestig** <u>zehs</u>·tihkh
70	**zeventig** <u>zay</u>·fuhn·tihkh
80	**tachtig** <u>tahkh</u>·tik
90	**negentig** <u>nay</u>·khuhn·tihkh
100	**honderd** <u>hohn</u>·duhrt
101	**honderdéén** <u>hohn</u>·duhrt·ayn
200	**tweehonderd** <u>tvay</u>·hohn·duhrt
500	**vijfhonderd** <u>fief</u>·hohn·duhrt
1,000	**duizend** <u>daw</u>·zuhnt
10,000	**tienduizend** <u>teen</u>·daw·zuhnt
1,000,000	**één miljoen** uhn mihl·<u>yoon</u>

Ordinal Numbers

first	**eerste**	ayr·stuh
second	**tweede**	tvay·duh
third	**derde**	dehr·duh
fourth	**vierde**	feer·duh
fifth	**vijfde**	fief·duh
once	**één keer**	ayn kayr
twice	**twee keer**	tvay kayr
three times	**drie keer**	dree kayr

Time ————————————————————

Essential

What time is it?	**Hoe laat is het?** hoo laat ihs heht
It's noon [midday].	**Het is twaalf uur 's middags.** heht ihs tvaalf ewr smih·dahkhs
At midnight.	**Om middernacht.** ohm mih·duhr·nahkht
From nine o'clock to 5 o'clock.	**Van negen tot vijf.** fahn nay·khuhn toht fief
Twenty after [past] four.	**Tien voor half vijf.** teen foar hahlf fief
A quarter to nine.	**Kwart voor negen.** kvahrt foar nay·khuhn
5:30 a.m./p.m.	**Half zes 's morgens/Half zes 's avonds.** hahlf zehs smohr·khuhns/hahlf zehs saa·fohnts

Days

Essential

Monday	**maandag** <u>maan</u>·dahkh
Tuesday	**dinsdag** <u>dihns</u>·dahkh
Wednesday	**woensdag** <u>voons</u>·dahkh
Thursday	**donderdag** <u>dohn</u>·duhr·dahkh
Friday	**vrijdag** <u>frie</u>·dahkh
Saturday	**zaterdag** <u>zaa</u>·tuhr·dahkh
Sunday	**zondag** <u>zohn</u>·dahkh

Dates

yesterday	**gisteren** <u>khihs</u>·tuh·ruhn
today	**vandaag** fahn·<u>daakh</u>
tomorrow	**morgen** <u>mohr</u>·khuhn
day	**dag** dahkh
week	**week** vayk
month	**maand** maant
year	**jaar** yaar

Months

January	**januari** <u>yah</u>·new·aa·ree
February	**februari** <u>fay</u>·brew·aa·ree
March	**maart** maart
April	**april** ah·<u>prihl</u>
May	**mei** mie
June	**juni** <u>yew</u>·nee
July	**juli** <u>yew</u>·lee
August	**augustus** ow·<u>khuhs</u>·tuhs
September	**september** sehp·<u>tehm</u>·buhr
October	**oktober** ohk·<u>toa</u>·buhr
November	**november** noa·<u>fehm</u>·buhr
December	**december** day·<u>sehm</u>·buhr

Seasons

spring	**de lente** duh <u>lehn</u>·tuh
summer	**de zomer** duh <u>zoa</u>·muhr
fall [autumn]	**de herfst** duh hehrfst
winter	**de winter** duh <u>vihn</u>·tuhr

Holidays

January 1 **Nieuwjaarsdag** New Year's Day

April 30 **Koninginnedag** Queen Mother's Birthday

May 4 **Dodenherdenking** Remembrance Day, World War II

May 5 **Bevrijdingsdag** Liberation Day

December 25 **Eerste kerstdag** Christmas Day

December 26 **Tweede kerstdag** Boxing Day

Movable Dates

Good Friday	**Goede Vrijdag**
Easter	**Pasen**
Ascension	**Hemelvaartsdag**
Pentecost	**Pinksteren**

Conversion Tables

When you know	Multiply by	To find
ounces	28.3	grams
pounds	0.45	kilograms
inches	2.54	centimeters
feet	0.3	meters
miles	1.61	kilometers
square inches	6.45	sq. centimeters
square feet	0.09	sq. meters
square miles	2.59	sq. kilometers
pints (U.S./Brit)	0.47/0.56	liters
gallons (U.S./Brit)	3.8/4.5	liters
Fahrenheit	5/9, after −32	Centigrade
Centigrade	9/5, then +32	Fahrenheit

Mileage

1 km − 0.62 mi	20 km − 12.4 mi
5 km − 3.10 mi	50 km − 31.0 mi
10 km − 6.20 mi	100 km − 61.0 mi

Measurement

1 gram	**gram** khrahm	= 0.035 oz.
1 kilogram (kg)	**kilogram** <u>kee</u>·loa·khrahm	= 2.2 lb
1 liter (l)	**liter** <u>lee</u>·tuhr	= 1.06 U.S./ 0.88 Brit. quarts
1 centimeter (cm)	**centimeter** <u>sehn</u>·tee· <u>may</u>·tuhr	= 0.4 inch
1 meter (m)	**meter** <u>may</u>·tuhr	= 3.28 feet
1 kilometer (km)	**kilometer** <u>kee</u>·loa·<u>may</u>·tuhr	= 0.62 mile

Temperature

-40° C − -40° F	-1° C − 30° F	20° C − 68° F
-30° C − -22° F	0° C − 32° F	25° C − 77° F
-20° C − -4° F	5° C − 41° F	30° C − 86° F
-10° C − 14° F	10° C − 50° F	35° C − 95° F
-5° C − 23° F	15° C − 59° F	

Oven Temperature

100° C − 212° F	177° C − 350° F
121° C − 250° F	204° C − 400° F
149° C − 300° F	260° C − 500° F

Useful Websites

www.holland.com
The Netherlands official tourism board

www.klm.com
KLM Royal Dutch Airlines website

www.ns.nl
The Netherlands Railways website

www.caa.co.uk
U.K. Civil Aviation Authority (CAA)

www.tsa.gov
U.S. Transportation Security Administration (TSA)

www.hihostels.com
Hostelling International website

English–Dutch Dictionary

A

about (approximately) ongeveer;
(regarding) over
above boven
abroad in het buitenland
accept accepteren
access toegang
accident ongeluk
accidentally per ongeluk
accommodations logies
accompany meegaan
acetaminophen paracetamol
acne acne
across naar de overkant
acupuncture acupunctuur
adapter adapter
additional extra
address adres
adjoining aangrenzend
admission charge toegangsprijs
adult volwassene
after na
afternoon middag
aftershave aftershave
agree akkoord gaan
air lucht
air conditioning airco
air mattress luchtbed

air pump luchtpomp
airmail luchtpost
airport vliegveld
airsickness luchtziekte
aisle gangpad
alarm clock wekker
all alle
allergic allergisch
allergy allergie
alley steegje
all-night pharmacy nachtapotheek
allow toestaan
allowance (quantity) toegestane
hoeveelheid; (permit) vergunning
almost bijna
alone alleen
already al
also ook
alter vermaken
alternate *adj* alternatief
aluminum foil aluminiumfolie
always altijd
amazing verbazingwekkend
ambassador ambassadeur
ambulance ambulance
American *n* Amerikaan;
adj Amerikaans
amount (money) bedrag;
(quantity) hoeveelheid
amusement park pretpark
anesthetic verdovingsmiddel
and en
anemia bloedarmoede

| **adj** | adjective | **adv** | adverb | **BE** | British English |
| **n** | noun | **v** | verb | | |

animal dier
another een ander
antacid antacidum
antibiotics antibiotica
antifreeze antivries
antique antiek
antiseptic *adj* antiseptisch
any wat
anyone iemand
anything iets
apartment appartement
apologize zich verontschuldigen
appendix blindedarm
appetite eetlust
appointment afspraak
approve goedkeuren
approximately ongeveer
arcade speelhal
area code netnummer
arm arm
aromatherapy aromatherapie
around rond
arrivals (airport) aankomst
arrive arriveren
art gallery kunstgalerie
arthritis artritis
ashtray asbak
ask vragen
aspirin aspirine
assistance hulp
asthma astma
at (time) om; (place) op
ATM geldautomaat
attack aanval
attractive aantrekkelijk
audio guide audiogids

aunt tante
Australia Australië
authentic authentiek
authenticity echtheid
automatic (car) automaat
available (seat) vrij;
  (general) beschikbaar
away *adv* weg
awful afschuwelijk

B

baby baby
baby bottle zuigfles
baby food babyvoeding
baby wipes babydoekjes
babysitter oppas
back (body part) rug;
  (not front) achterkant
backache rugpijn
backpack rugzak
bad slecht
bag tas
baggage [BE] bagage
baggage claim bagageafhaalruimte
bake bakken
bakery bakker
balcony balkon
ball bal
ballet ballet
band band
bandage (small) pleister;
  (large) verband
bank bank
bank charges bankkosten
bar bar
barber herenkapper

bargain koopje
barrier barrière
baseball honkbal
basement kelder
basket mand
basketball basketbal
bath bad
bathroom (bath/shower) badkamer; **(restroom)** toilet
battery (general) batterij; **(car)** accu
battlesite slagveld
be zijn
beach strand
beautiful mooi
because omdat
become worden
bed bed
bed and breakfast logies en ontbijt
bedding beddengoed
bedroom slaapkamer
before voor
begin beginnen
beginner beginner
behind achter
Belgium België
belong toebehoren
belt riem
bet wedden
between tussen
beware oppassen
bib slabbetje
bicycle fiets
big groot
bike path fietspad
bikini bikini

bill *n* rekening
binoculars verrekijker
bird vogel
birthday verjaardag
bite (general) beet; **(insect)** beet; *v* bijten
bitter bitter
bizarre bizar
bladder blaas
blanket deken
bleach bleekmiddel
bleed bloeden
blister blaar
blocked (drain) verstopt; **(road)** versperd
blood bloed
blood group bloedgroep
blood pressure bloeddruk
blouse bloes
blow dry föhnen
blue blauw
board *v* boarden
boarding card instapkaart
boat trip boottocht
bone bot
book boek
bookstore boekwinkel
boots laarzen
boring saai
born geboren
borrow lenen
botanical garden botanische tuin
bother *v* lastigvallen
bottle fles
bottle opener flesopener
boulevard boulevard

bowel darm
bowl kom
box doos
boxing boksen
boy jongen
boyfriend vriend
bra beha
bracelet armband
brake rem
break *v* breken
break down (car) pech hebben;
　(appliance) defect raken
breakfast ontbijt
breast borst
breastfeed borst geven
breathe ademhalen
bridge brug
bring brengen
British *n* Britten; *adj* Brits
brochure brochure
broken (body part or thing)
　gebroken; **(thing)** kapot
bronchitis bronchitis
brooch broche
broom bezem
bruise blauwe plek
bucket emmer
bug insect
building gebouw
build *v* bouwen
bulletin board mededelingenbord
burn brandwond
bus bus
bus lane busbaan
bus route busroute
bus shelter bushokje
bus station busstation

bus stop bushalte
bus ticket strippenkaart
business zaken
business card visitekaartje
business center bedrijvencomplex
business class businessclass
business district zakendistrict
busy druk
but maar
butane gas butagas
butcher slager
button knoop
buy kopen
by (near) bij; **(time)** niet later dan
bye (also used at arrival) dag;
　(only at departure) tot ziens

C

cabin hut
cafe café
calendar kalender
call *n* gesprek; **(phone)** *v* bellen;
　(name) *v* heten
calorie calorie
camera fototoestel
camp *v* kamperen
campsite camping
can (may) mogen;
　(be able) kunnen
can opener blikopener
Canada Canada
canal (general) kanaal;
　(in city) gracht
cancel annuleren
cancer kanker
candle kaars

canoeing kanovaren
cap (hat) pet; **(dental)** kroon
capsule (medication) capsule
car (vehicle) auto;
(train compartment) wagon
car deck (ferry) autodek
car hire [BE] autoverhuurbedrijf
car park [BE] parkeerplaats
car rental autoverhuurbedrijf
car seat kinderzitje
card kaart
careful voorzichtig
carpet tapijt
carry-on luggage handbagage
cart wagentje
carton doos
cash adv contant; v verzilveren
cash register kassa
casino casino
castle kasteel
catch pakken; **(bus)** nemen
cathedral kathedraal
caution oppassen
cave grot
CD cd
CD player cd-speler
cell phone (informal) mobiel;
(formal) mobiele telefoon
cemetery begraafplaats
ceramics keramiek
certificate certificaat
change (money) n wisselgeld;
(buses) v overstappen; **(money)**
v wisselen; **(reservation)**
v veranderen; **(baby)** v verschonen
charcoal houtskool
charge n prijs; v berekenen

cheap goedkoop
check n rekening; v checken
check in inchecken
check out (hotel) uitchecken
checking account betaalrekening
cheers proost
chemical toilet chemisch toilet
chemist [BE] (with prescriptions)
apotheek; **(without prescriptions)**
drogisterij
cheque [BE] rekening
chest borstkas
child kind
child seat kinderstoeltje
child's cot [BE] wieg
children's clothing kinderkleding
children's menu kindermenu
children's portion kinderportie
choose selecteren
church kerk
cigarette sigaret
cigar sigaar
cinema [BE] bioscoop
class klas
clean schoon
cleaning supplies
schoonmaakmiddelen
clearance opruiming
cliff klif
cling film [BE] huishoudfolie
clinic kliniek
clock klok
clog n klomp
close adv dichtbij; v sluiten
clothing store kledingwinkel
cloudy bewolkt

club club
coast kust
coat jas
coat check garderobe
coat hanger kleerhanger
code code
coin munt
cold (chilly) koud; (flu) verkoudheid
collapse instorten
colleague collega
collect ophalen
collection (mail) lichting
color kleur
comb kam
come komen
commission commissie
compact compact
company (business) bedrijf;
  (companionship) gezelschap
compartment (train) coupé
computer computer
concert concert
concert hall concertgebouw
concession concessie
concussion hersenschudding
conditioner conditioner
condom condoom
conductor dirigent
conference conferentie
confirm bevestigen
congratulations gefeliciteerd
connect verbinding maken
connection verbinding
conscious bewust
conservation area beschermd
  natuurgebied

constant constant
constipation constipatie
consulate consulaat
consult raadplegen
contact bereiken
contact lens contactlens
contact lens solution
  contactlensvloeistof
contagious besmettelijk
contain bevatten
contemporary modern
contest wedstrijd
continuous doorlopend
contraceptive voorbehoedsmiddel
contribution bijdrage
control controle
convention congres
convention hall congresgebouw
cook n kok; v koken
cooker [BE] fornuis
cooking (cuisine) keuken
cooking facilities kookgelegenheid
cool (cold) koel; (nice) cool
copper koper
copy n kopie; v kopiëren
corkscrew kurkentrekker
corner hoek
correct correct
cosmetic cosmetisch
cost kosten
costume (local) klederdracht
cot ledikant
cottage vakantiehuisje
cotton katoen
cough n hoest; v hoesten
could kunnen

counter (shop) toonbank
country land
country code landnummer
courier koerier
course (meal) gang;
 (medication) kuur
courthouse rechtbank
cousin (male) neef; **(female)** nicht
cover charge couvert
craft shop handwerkwinkel
cramps kramp
credit card creditcard
crib wieg
cross *n* kruis; *v* oversteken
crossing overtocht
crosswalk zebrapad
crowded vol
crown (dental) kroon
cruise *n* cruise; *v* cruisen
crutches krukken
crystal kristal
cup kopje
currency valuta
currency exchange office
 geldwisselkantoor
curtain gordijn
curve bocht
custom made op maat gemaakt
customer information
 klanteninformatie
customer service klantenservice
customs douane
customs declaration form
 douaneaangifteformulier
cut *n* snijwond; *v* knippen
cute schattig

cycle route fietsroute
cycling fietsen
cycling race wielerwedstrijd

D

daily dagelijks
dairy zuivel
dairy products zuivelproducten
damage schade
damaged beschadigd
damp vochtig
dance *n* dans; *v* dansen
dance club discotheek
dangerous gevaarlijk
dark donker
date of birth geboortedatum
dawn dageraad
day dag
day trip dagtocht
dead end doodlopende weg
deaf doof
deck chair ligstoel
declare aangeven
decorative decoratief
decorative tile siertegel
deep diep
defrost ontdooien
degree graad
delay vertraging
delete verwijderen
Delft blue Delfts blauw
delicatessen delicatessen
delicious heerlijk
deliver (give birth) bevallen;
 (bring) afleveren

delivery levering
denim spijkerstof
dental floss floss
dental office tandartspraktijk
dentist tandarts
denture kunstgebit
deodorant deodorant
depart vertrekken
department store warenhuis
departure gate vertrekgate
departure lounge vertrekhal
departures vertrek
deposit *n* borgsom
describe beschrijven
destination bestemming
detail detail
detergent wasmiddel
detour omleiding
develop ontwikkelen
diabetes diabetes
diabetic *adj* diabetisch;
    n suikerpatiënt
dial (phone) *v* kiezen
diamond diamant
diaper luier
diarrhea diarree
diabetic suikerpatiënt
dice dobbelsteen
dictionary woordenboek
diesel diesel
diet dieet
difficult moeilijk
digital digitaal
dine dineren
dining car restauratiewagen
dining room eetkamer

dinner avondeten
direct *adj* rechtstreeks; *v* de weg
    wijzen
direction richting
directions (map) aanwijzingen
directory (phone) telefoonboek
dirty vies
disabled gehandicapt
disconnect verbinding verbreken
discount korting
discount store discountzaak
dish (plate) bord; (food) gerecht
dishwasher afwasmachine
dishwashing liquid afwasmiddel
dislocate ontwrichten
display case vitrine
disposable wegwerpbaar
dissolve oplossen
distance afstand
disturb storen
dive duiken
diving equipment duikapparatuur
divorce scheiden
dizzy duizelig
do doen
dock dok
doctor dokter
dog hond
doll pop
dollar (U.S.) dollar
domestic binnenlands
donation gift
door deur
dosage dosering
double dubbel
double room tweepersoonskamer

downstairs beneden
downtown stadscentrum
dozen dozijn
dress n jurk; v aankleden
dress code kledingvoorschriften
drink n drankje; v drinken
drip druppelen
drive rijden
driver chauffeur
driver's license rijbewijs
drop (medicine) druppel
drown verdrinken
drowsy suf
drowsiness sufheid
drugstore drogisterij
drunk dronken
dry droog
dry clean stomen
dry cleaner stomerij
dubbed nagesynchroniseerd
dummy [BE] fopspeen
during tijdens
Dutch (language) Nederlands;
  (people) Nederlanders
duty (tax) accijns
duty-free belastingvrij

E

ear oor
ear drops oordruppels
earache oorpijn
early vroeg
earrings oorbellen
east oost
easy makkelijk

eat eten
economy class (general) economy
  class; **(train)** tweede klas
electrical outlet stopcontact
electronic elektronisch
elevator n lift
e-mail e-mail
e-mail address e-mailadres
embassy ambassade
emerald smaragd
emergency noodgeval
emergency brake noodrem
emergency exit nooduitgang
emergency service hulpdienst
empty adj leeg; v leegmaken
end n einde; v aflopen
engaged (marriage) verloofd
England Engeland
English Engels
English-speaking Engelstalig
engrave graveren
enjoy leuk vinden
enlarge vergroten
enough genoeg
entertainment guide uitgids
entrance ingang
entrance fee toegangsprijs
entrance ramp (highway) oprit
  snelweg
entry ingang
entry visa inreisvisum
envelope envelop
epileptic epileptisch
equipment (clothing) uitrusting;
  (machine) apparatuur
error fout

escalator roltrap
essential essentieel
e-ticket e-ticket
euro euro
Eurocheque Eurocheque
evening avond
event evenement
every elk
exact exact
examination onderzoek
example voorbeeld
except uitgezonderd
excess luggage overbagage
exchange (general) ruilen;
  (money) wisselen
exchange rate wisselkoers
excursion excursie
exhausted uitgeput
exit (door) uitgang;
  (highway) afslag
exit ramp afrit
expensive duur
experience ervaring
expiration date vervaldatum
expose blootstellen
express mail per expres
extension (phone) toestel
extra (additional) extra
extract *v* onttrekken
eye oog
eyebrow wenkbrauw

F

fabric stof
face gezicht
facial *n* gezichtsbehandeling

facilities faciliteiten
factor factor
faint *adj* zwak; *v* flauwvallen
fall *v* vallen
family (immediate) gezin;
  (relatives) familie
famous beroemd
fan *n* ventilator
far ver
far-sighted verziend
farm boerderij
fast (speedy) snel; (clock) loopt
  voor
fast food fastfood
faucet kraan
faulty defect
favorite favoriet
fax fax
fax machine faxapparaat
fax number faxnummer
feature kenmerk
feed voeden
feel voelen
female vrouwelijk
ferry veerboot
fever koorts
few weinig
fiancé verloofde
field weiland
fight *n* gevecht; *v* vechten
fill vullen
fill out invullen
fill up opvullen
filling vulling
film (movie) film;
  (camera) fotorolletje

filter filter
find vinden
fine (good) goed; **(well)** prima;
(police) boete
finger vinger
fire (campfire) kampvuur;
(disaster) brand
fire alarm brandalarm
fire brigade [BE] brandweer
fire department brandweer
fire door branddeur
fire escape nooduitgang
fire exit brandtrap
fire extinguisher brandblusser
first eerst
first class eerste klas
fishing *v* vissen
fit passen
fitting room paskamer
fix (repair) repareren
flash flits
flashlight zaklantaarn
flavor smaak
flea market vlooienmarkt
flight vlucht
flight attendant (male) steward;
(female) stewardess
flight number vluchtnummer
floor (level) verdieping
florist bloemenwinkel
flower bloem
flu griep
flush doorspoelen
fly *n* vlieg; *v* vliegen
fog mist
follow volgen

food voedsel
food poisoning voedselvergiftiging
foot voet
footpath [BE] voetpad
football [BE] voetbal
for voor
for sale te koop
foreign buitenlands
forest bos
forget vergeten
fork vork
form *n* formulier
formal dress avondkleding
formula (baby) flesvoeding
fountain fontein
fracture breuk
frame (glasses) montuur
free (available) vrij
free of charge gratis
freeze bevriezen
freezer diepvriezer
frequent *adj* vaak
fresh vers
friend vriend
from (general) van;
(destination) uit
front voorkant
frying pan koekenpan
fuel (gas) benzine
full vol
fun plezier
funny grappig
furniture meubels
fuse zekering
fuse box zekeringkast

G

gallery galerie
game (competition) wedstrijd; **(tennis)** game; **(toy)** spelletje
garage garage
garbage bag vuilniszak
garden tuin
gas (gasoline) benzine
gas station benzinestation
gas tank benzinetank
gate (airport) gate; **(general)** hek
gauze gaas
gear versnelling
genuine echt
get (receive) krijgen
get off (bus) uitstappen
gift cadeau
gift store cadeauwinkel
girl meisje
girlfriend vriendin
give geven
glass (drinking) glas
glasses (optical) bril
gloves handschoenen
gluten gluten
go gaan
goggles duikbril
gold goud
golf golf
golf club golfstok
golf course golfbaan
good goed
goodbye dag
gram gram
grass gras

great prima
Great Britain Groot-Brittannië
green groen
greengrocer [BE] groenteman
groundcloth grondzeil
groundsheet [BE] grondzeil
group groep
guarantee garantie
guesthouse pension
guide (tour) gids
guide book gids
guide dog geleidehond
guided tour rondleiding
guided walk begeleide wandeling
guitar gitaar
gym fitnessruimte

H

hair haar
hairbrush borstel
hairdresser dameskapper
halal halal
half *n* helft; *adj* halve
hammer hamer
hand hand
hand luggage handbagage
hand washable met de hand wassen
handbag [BE] handtas
handicapped gehandicapt
handicrafts ambachten
handkerchief zakdoek
hanger klerenhanger
hangover kater
happen gebeuren
happy blij

harbor haven
hard (tough) hard;
  (difficult) moeilijk
hardware store ijzerwarenwinkel
hat hoed
have hebben
hay fever hooikoorts
head hoofd
headache hoofdpijn
health gezondheid
health food reformproducten
health food store reformwinkel
health insurance
  ziektekostenverzekering
hear horen
hearing aid gehoorapparaat
hearing impaired slechthorend
heart hart
heart attack hartaanval
heart condition hartkwaal
heat verwarming
heating [BE] verwarming
heavy zwaar
height (person) lengte;
  (general) hoogte
hello hallo
helmet helm
help helpen
her haar
here hier
hi hallo
high hoog
highchair kinderstoel
highway snelweg
hiking wandelen
hiking gear wandeluitrusting

hill heuvel
hire huren
historical historisch
hobby hobby
hold (general) vasthouden;
  (phone) aan de lijn blijven
hole gat
holiday [BE] vakantie
home (place) thuis; **(direction)**
  naar huis
homemade zelfgemaakt
honeymoon huwelijksreis
horn claxon
horse paard
horseback riding paardrijden
horsetrack paardenrenbaan
hospital ziekenhuis
hot heet
hotel hotel
hour uur
house huis
how hoe
how much hoeveel
how many hoeveel
hug omhelzen
hunger honger
hungry hongerig
hunt jagen
hurry *n* haast; *v* haasten
hurt *n* pijn; *v* pijn hebben
husband man

I

I ik
ibuprofen ibuprofen
ice-cream parlor ijssalon

ice hockey ijshockey
ice skating schaatsen
identification legitimatiebewijs
ill [BE] ziek
illegal illegaal
imitation imitatie
important belangrijk
improve verbeteren
in in
incline helling
include bevatten
indigestion indigestie
indoor pool binnenbad
inexpensive goedkoop
infect ontsteken
infection infectie
inflammation ontsteking
informal informeel
information (general) informatie;
  (phone inquiry) inlichtingen
information desk informatiebalie
injection injectie
injure verwonden
innocent onschuldig
insect insect
insect bite insectenbeet
insect repellent insectenspray
insert (ATM) invoeren
inside binnen
insist aandringen
insomnia slapeloosheid
instant messenger instant
  messenger
instead of in plaats van
instructions gebruiksaanwijzing
instructor instructeur

insulin insuline
insurance verzekering
insurance card verzekeringsbewijs
insurance certificate [BE]
  verzekeringsbewijs
insurance claim schadeclaim
interest (hobby) interesse
interference storing
intermission pauze
international internationaal
International Student Card
  Internationale Studentenkaart
internet internet
internet cafe internetcafé
internet service internetverbinding
interpreter tolk
intersection kruispunt
into naar
introduce (person) voorstellen
invite uitnodigen
iodine jodium
Ireland Ierland
iron *n* strijkijzer
is is
itch jeuk
item ding
itemized gespecificeerd

J

jacket jasje
jar pot
jaw kaak
jeans spijkerbroek
jet lag jetlag
jet-ski jetski

jeweler juwelier
jewelry sieraden
job baan
join meedoen
joint *adj* gezamenlijk; *n* gewricht
joke grap
journey reis

K

keep houden
keep out verboden toegang
key sleutel
key card sleutelkaart
key ring sleutelring
kiddie pool kinderbadje
kidney nier
kilo kilo
kilometer kilometer
kind (pleasant) aardig; (type) soort
kiss *v* kussen
kitchen keuken
knee knie
knife mes
knock kloppen
know kennen
kosher koosjer

L

label label
lace kant
lactose intolerant lactose-intolerant
ladder ladder
lake meer
lamp lamp
land *n* land; *v* landen

lane (traffic) rijstrook;
  (path) laantje
language course taalcursus
large groot
last (end) *adj* laatst; (previous)
  adj vorige; (keep) *v* meegaan
late (delayed) vertraagd
launderette [BE] wasserette
laundromat wasserette
laundry service wasserij
laundry facilities wasmachines
lawyer advocaat
laxative laxerend middel
lead (road) gaan naar
leader (group) groepsleider
leak lekken
learn leren
leather leer
leave (depart) vertrekken;
  (deposit) betalen;
  (forget something) vergeten
left links
left-luggage office [BE] bagagedepot
leg (body part) been
legal legaal
lend lenen
length lengte
lens lens
lens cap lensdop
less minder
lesson les
let laten
letter brief
level *adj* gelijk; *n* verdieping
library bibliotheek
life leven

life boat reddingsboot
life guard (pool) badmeester; (beach) strandmeester
life jacket reddingsvest
lift [BE] lift
light licht
lightbulb gloeilamp
lighthouse vuurtoren
lighter *adj* lichter; *n* aansteker
line lijn
linen linnen
lip lip
lipstick lippenstift
liquor store slijter
liter liter
little klein
live wonen
liver lever
living room woonkamer
loafers instappers
lobby (theater, hotel) hal
local plaatselijk
lock *n* slot; *v* afsluiten
log on inloggen
log off uitloggen
long lang
long-distance bus touringcar
long-sighted [BE] verziend
look *n* stijl; *v* kijken
loose los
lorry [BE] vrachtauto
lose verliezen
lost (misplaced) verloren; (direction) verdwaald
lost-and-found gevonden voorwerpen

lost property office [BE] gevonden voorwerpen
lottery loterij
loud (general) luid; (voice) hard
love *n* liefde; (general) *v* dol zijn op; (romantic) *v* houden van
low laag
luggage bagage
luggage cart bagagewagentje
luggage trolley [BE] bagagewagentje
lump gezwel
lunch lunch
lung long

M

machine washable in de machine wassen
madam mevrouw
magazine tijdschrift
magnificent magnifiek
mail *n* post; *v* posten
mailbox brievenbus
main grootste
make-up make-up
male mannelijk
mall winkelcentrum
mallet houten hamer
man man
manager manager
mandatory verplicht
manicure manicure
many veel
map kaart
market markt
marry trouwen
mascara mascara

mask masker
mass mis
massage massage
matches lucifers
matinee matinee
mattress matras
maybe misschien
meal maaltijd
mean v betekenen
measure meten
measurement afmeting
measuring cup maatbeker
measuring spoon maatlepel
mechanic monteur
medication medicijn
medicine geneesmiddel
meet ontmoeten
meeting vergadering
meeting room vergaderruimte
meeting place ontmoetingsplaats
member lid
memorial gedenkteken
memory card geheugenkaart
mend (clothes) verstellen
menstrual cramps menstruatiepijn
menu menukaart
merge (traffic) invoegen
message bericht
metal metaal
microwave (oven) magnetron
midday [BE] twaalf uur 's middags
midnight middernacht
migraine migraine
mini-bar minibar
minute minuut
mirror spiegel

missing kwijt
mistake fout
mobile home camper
mobile phone [BE]
  (informal) mobiel;
  (formal) mobiele telefoon
moisturizer (cream)
  vochtinbrengende crème
money geld
money order postwissel
month maand
mop dweil
moped brommer
more meer
morning ochtend
mosque moskee
mosquito bite muggenbeet
motion sickness reisziekte
motor motor
motor boat motorboot
motorcycle motorfiets
motorway [BE] snelweg
mountain berg
mountain bike mountainbike
moustache snor
mouth mond
move (general) bewegen;
  (relocate) verhuizen
movie film
movie theater bioscoop
Mr. De heer (Dhr.); meneer
Mrs. Mevrouw (Mevr.)
much veel
mugging beroving
mug mok
muscle spier

museum museum
music muziek
must moeten

N

nail nagel
nail file nagelvijl
nail salon nagelsalon
name naam
napkin servet
nappy [BE] luier
narrow smal
national nationaal
nationality nationaliteit
native inwoner
nature natuur
nature reserve natuurreservaat
nature trail natuurpad
nausea misselijkheid
nauseous misselijk
near dichtbij
nearby in de buurt
nearest dichtstbijzijnde
near-sighted bijziend
necessary nodig
neck nek
necklace halsketting
need v nodig hebben
network netwerk
never nooit
new nieuw
New Zealand Nieuw-Zeeland
news nieuws
news agent [BE] kiosk
newspaper krant
newsstand kiosk

next volgende
next to naast
nice fijn
night nacht
night club nachtclub
no (denial) nee; **(prohibition)** niet
no parking parkeerverbod
noisy lawaaierig
non-EU citizens niet-EU-ingezetenen
non-smoking niet-roken
non-stop non-stop
noon twaalf uur 's middags
normal normaal
north noord
nose neus
not niet
nothing niets
notify informeren
now nu
number nummer
nurse verpleegster
nylon nylon

O

o'clock uur
office kantoor
office hours kantooruren
office supplies kantoorbenodigdheden
off-licence [BE] slijter
off-peak (ticket) daluren
office kantoor
often vaak
oil olie
OK oké

old oud
on op
once één keer
one-way (traffic) eenrichtingsverkeer
one-way ticket enkeltje
only slechts
open *adj* open; **(shop)** *v* opengaan; **(window)** *v* opendoen
opening hours [BE] openingstijden
opera opera
operation operatie
opposite tegenover
opticien opticiën
or of
orally oraal
orchestra orkest
order bestellen
organize organiseren
original origineel
out uit
outdoor *adj* openlucht
outdoor pool buitenbad
outside buiten
oval ovaal
oven oven
over (more than) meer dan
overcharged teveel betaald
overheat oververhit worden
overlook uitkijkpunt
overnight in één nacht
owe verschuldigd zijn
own *adj* eigen; *v* bezitten
owner eigenaar

P

pacifier fopspeen
pack inpakken
package pakje
paddling pool [BE] kinderzwembad
padlock hangslot
pail emmer
pain pijn
paint *v* verven
painting schilderij
pair paar
pajamas pyjama
palace paleis
palpitations hartkloppingen
panorama panorama
pants lange broek
panty hose panty
paper towel keukenpapier
paracetamol [BE] paracetamol
paralysis verlamming
parcel [BE] pak
parents ouders
park *n* park; *v* parkeren
parking garage parkeergarage
parking lot parkeerplaats
parking meter parkeermeter
parking ticket parkeerbon
partner partner
part time parttime
party (social) feestje
pass (a place) langskomen; **(traffic)** inhalen
passenger passagier
passport paspoort
password wachtwoord

pastry store banketbakker
patient *adj* geduldig; *n* patiënt
pavement [BE] stoep
pay phone telefoonzuil
pay betalen
payment betaling
pearl parel
pedestrian voetganger
pedestrian crossing
  voetgangersoversteekplaats
pedestrian zone verkeersvrij gebied
pediatrician kinderarts
pedicure pedicure
peg wasknijper
pen pen
penicillin penicilline
per per
performance voorstelling
perhaps misschien
period (general) periode;
  (menstrual) menstruatie
person persoon
petite tenger
petrol [BE] benzine
petrol station [BE] benzinestation
pewter tin
pharmacy apotheek
phone *n* telefoon; *v* telefoneren
phone call telefoongesprek
phone card telefoonkaart
phone directory telefoongids
phone number telefoonnummer
photocopy *n* kopie; *v* kopiëren
photograph foto
photography fotografie
phrase zinsnede

phrase book taalgids
pick up *v* ophalen
picnic picknick
picnic area picknickplaats
piece stuk
pill pil
pillow kussen
PIN PIN
pipe (smoking) pijp
pizzeria pizzeria
place plaats
plane vliegtuig
plan plan
plaster [BE] pleister
plastic plastic
plastic wrap huishoudfolie
plate bord
platform spoor
platinum platina
play *n* toneelstuk; *v* spelen
playground speeltuin
playpen babybox
pleasant prettig
please alstublieft
plug plug
plunger ontstopper
pneumonia longontsteking
poison gif
police politie
police report proces-verbaal
police station politiebureau
pollen count stuifmeelgehalte
polyester polyester
pond vijver
pool zwembad
popular populair

porcelain porselein
port (harbor) haven
porter kruier
portion portie
post [BE] *n* post; *v* versturen
post office postkantoor
postage posttarief
postbox [BE] brievenbus
postcard ansichtkaart
pot pot
pottery aardewerk
pound pond
pound sterling Britse pond
power (electricity) stroom
practice praktijk
pregnant zwanger
premium (gas) super
prepaid phone card prepaidkaart
prescription recept
present *n* cadeau; *v* geven
press persen
pretty mooi
price prijs
print afdrukken
prison gevangenis
private particulier
produce store groentewinkel
profession beroep
problem probleem
prohibited verboden
program programma
pronounce uitspreken
pub pub
public *n* publiek; *adj* openbaar
pull trekken
pump pomp

pure zuiver
purpose doel
purse (handbag) handtas
push duwen
pushchair [BE] kinderwagen
put neerzetten

Q

quality kwaliteit
quarter kwart
queue [BE] *n* rij; *v* in de rij staan
quick snel
quiet rustig

R

racetrack circuit
racket (tennis) racket
railroad crossing overweg
railway station [BE] station
rain *n* regen; *v* regenen
raincoat regenjas
rape verkrachting
rapids stroomversnelling
rash uitslag
razor scheerapparaat
reach bereiken
reaction reactie
read lezen
ready klaar
real (genuine) echt
receipt (in shop) bon;
  (formal) kwitantie
receive ontvangen
reception (desk) receptie
receptionist receptionist

recommend aanbevelen
reduce verminderen
reduction korting
refrigerator koelkast
refund *n* terugbetaling;
  v terugbetalen
region streek
registered mail aangetekende post
registration form inschrijfformulier
regular normaal
relationship relatie
reliable betrouwbaar
religion godsdienst
remember (recall) herinneren;
  (not forget) onthouden
remove verwijderen
renovation renovatie
rent *n* huur; *v* huren
rental car huurauto
repair repareren
repeat herhalen
replace vervangen
replacement part
  vervangingsonderdeel
report *n* rapport; *v* melden
required vereist
reservation reservering
reservation desk reserveringsbalie
reserve reserveren
reservoir reservoir
responsibility verantwoordelijkheid
rest rusten
rest area rustgebied
restaurant restaurant
restroom toilet
retired gepensioneerd

return ticket [BE] retourtje
right (correct) juist;
  (direction) rechts
ring ring
river rivier
road weg
road map wegenkaart
roadwork wegwerkzaamheden
rob beroven
robbery beroving
rock rots
romantic romantisch
roof dak
room kamer
room service roomservice
rope touw
rose roos
round rond
round-trip ticket retourtje
route route
row roeien
rowboat roeiboot
rubbish [BE] vuilnis
rude onbeleefd
ruins ruïne
rush haasten

S

safe *adj* veilig; *n* kluis
safety veiligheid
safety pin veiligheidsspeld
sale opruiming
sales tax BTW
same hetzelfde
sand zand

sandals sandalen
sanitary napkin maandverband
sanitary pad [BE] maandverband
satin satijn
saucepan steelpan
sauna sauna
save (computer) opslaan
savings account spaarrekening
say zeggen
scarf sjaal
scissors schaar
Scotland Schotland
screwdriver schroevendraaier
sea zee
seasick zeeziek
season ticket abonnement
seat (on train, etc.) plaats
seat belt veiligheidsgordel
sedative kalmerend middel
see zien
self-service zelfbediening
sell verkopen
seminar seminar
send versturen
senior citizen oudere
separated uit elkaar
separate apart
serious ernstig
serve opdienen
service (church) kerkdienst;
  (restaurant) bediening
service charge bedieningsgeld
service included bediening
  inbegrepen
set menu dagmenu
sew naaien

sex seks
shadow schaduw
shallow ondiep
shampoo shampoo
shape vorm
share delen
sharp scherp
shave scheren
shaving brush scheerkwast
shaving cream scheerzeep
sheet (bed) laken
ship schip
shirt (men's) overhemd
shock schok
shoe schoen
shoe repair schoenmaker
shoe store schoenenwinkel
shop assistant winkelbediende
shopping *n* boodschappen;
  v winkelen
shopping basket winkelmandje
shopping centre
  [BE] winkelcentrum
shopping mall winkelcentrum
shopping cart winkelwagentje
shopping trolley
  [BE] winkelwagentje
short kort
short-sighted [BE] bijziend
shorts korte broek
shoulder schouder
shovel schep
show tonen
shower douche
shut *v* sluiten
shutter luik

sick (general) ziek;
  (nauseous) misselijk
side effect bijwerking
sidewalk stoep
sight (attraction)
  bezienswaardigheid
sightseeing tour toeristische rondrit
sign (road) n verkeersbord;
  (place signature) v tekenen
silk zijde
silver zilver
single (person) single
single ticket [BE] (travel) enkeltje
single room eenpersoonskamer
sink (bathroom) wastafel;
  (kitchen) gootsteen
sit zitten
site plaats
size maat
skating rink ijsbaan
skin huid
skirt rok
sleep slapen
sleeping bag slaapzak
sleeping car slaapwagen
sleeping pill slaappil
sleeve mouw
slice plak
slippers pantoffels
slow langzaam
small klein
smell geur
smoke roken
smoking area rokerszone
snack snack
snack bar snackbar

sneakers gymschoenen
snorkle snorkelen
snow n sneeuw; v sneeuwen
soap zeep
soccer voetbal
socket stopcontact
socks sokken
sold out uitverkocht
some enkele
someone iemand
something iets
sometimes soms
somewhere ergens
soon gauw
soother [BE] fopspeen
sore pijnlijk
sore throat keelpijn
sorry sorry
south zuid
souvenir souvenir
souvenir guide souvenirgids
souvenir store souvenirwinkel
spa kuuroord
space ruimte
spare extra
spatula spatel
speak spreken
special speciaal
specialist specialist
specimen monster
speed snelheid
speed limit snelheidslimiet
spell v spellen
spend uitgeven
sponge spons
spoon lepel

sport sport
sporting goods store sportwinkel
sports club sportvereniging
spot (place, site) plaats
spouse (male) echtgenoot;
  (female) echtgenote
sprain n verstuiking; v verstuiken
square vierkant
stadium stadion
staff personeel
stainless steel roestvrij staal
stairs trap
stamp n postzegel; v stempelen
stand staan
standard standaard
standby ticket standby-ticket
start (general) beginnen;
  (car, etc.) starten
statue standbeeld
stay n verblijf; **(remain)** v blijven;
  (overnight) v logeren
steal stelen
steel staal
steep steil
sterilizing solution steriele oplossing
sterling silver sterling zilver
stiff stijf
still nog
stolen gestolen
stomach maag
stomachache maagpijn
stop n halte; v stoppen
store winkel
store directory [BE]
  winkelplattegrond
store guide winkelplattegrond

stove fornuis
straight recht
stream beekje
street straat
stroller kinderwagen
strong sterk
student student
study studeren
stunning verbluffend
style n stijl; v stylen
subtitled ondertiteld
suburb buitenwijk
subway metro
subway map metrokaart
subway station metrostation
suggest voorstellen
suit pak
suitable geschikt
suitcase koffer
sun zon
sunbathe zonnebaden
sunblock sunblock
sunburn zonnebrand
sunglasses zonnebril
sunshade [BE] parasol
sunscreen zonnebrandcrème
suntan lotion zonnebrandcrème
super (petrol) [BE] super
superb voortreffelijk
supermarket supermarkt
supervision toezicht
suppository zetpil
surcharge toeslag
sure zeker
surfboard surfplank
swallow doorslikken

sweater trui
sweatshirt sweatshirt
sweep vegen
sweet zoet
swelling zwelling
swim zwemmen
swimsuit zwempak
swimming pool zwembad
swimming trunks zwembroek
swollen opgezet
symbol symbool
symptom symptoom
synagogue synagoge
synthetic synthetisch

T

T-shirt T-shirt
TV tv
table tafel
tablet tablet
take (general) nemen;
  (carry) meenemen;
  (medicine) innemen; (time) duren
take off (plane) opstijgen;
  (shoes) uitdoen
talk praten
tall lang
tampon tampon
tap [BE] kraan
taste n smaak; v proeven
taxi taxi
taxi rank [BE] taxistandplaats
taxi stand taxistandplaats
teaspoon theelepel
team team
tear (muscle) scheuren

tear off afscheuren
telephone n telefoon; v telefoneren
telephone booth telefoonzuil
telephone call telefoongesprek
telephone number telefoonnummer
tell vertellen
temperature temperatuur
tennis tennis
tennis court tennisbaan
tent tent
tent peg tentharing
tent pole tentstok
terminal terminal
terrible vreselijk
text n tekst
text messaging sms'en
thank danken
that dat
theater theater
theft diefstal
then (time) dan
there daar
thermometer thermometer
thermos thermosfles
these deze
thick dik
thief dief
thigh dij
thin dun
thing ding
think denken
thirsty dorstig
this dit
those die
throat keel
through door

thumb duim
ticket kaartje
ticket inspector conducteur
ticket office loket
tie n stropdas
tight krap
tile tegel
time tijd
timetable [BE] dienstregeling
tip fooi
tire band
tired moe
tissue tissue
to (place) naar
tobacco tabak
tobacconist sigarenwinkel
today vandaag
toe teen
toilet [BE] toilet
toilet paper toiletpapier
toll tol
toll booth tolhuisje
toll road tolweg
tomorrow morgen
tongue tong
tonight vanavond
too te
tooth tand
toothache kiespijn
toothbrush tandenborstel
toothpaste tandpasta
top bovenkant
torn gescheurd
tour excursie
tour guide reisgids
tourist toerist

tourist office VVV-kantoor
tournament toernooi
tow truck takelwagen
towel handdoek
tower toren
town stad
town hall stadhuis
town map stadsplattegrond
town square stadsplein
toy speelgoed
toy store speelgoedwinkel
traditional traditioneel
traffic verkeer
traffic circle rotonde
traffic jam file
traffic light stoplicht
traffic offence [BE] verkeersovertreding
traffic violation verkeersovertreding
trail wandelpad
trailer aanhangwagen
train trein
train station station
tram tram
transfer overstappen
transport vervoer
translate vertalen
translation vertaling
translator vertaler
trash vuilnis
trash can vuilnisbak
travel reizen
travel agency reisbureau
travel sickness reisziekte
traveler's check reischeque
traveller's cheque [BE] reischeque

tray plateau
treatment behandeling
tree boom
trim bijknippen
trip reis
trolley wagentje
trousers [BE] lange broek
truck vrachtwagen
true waar
try on (clothes) passen
tumor tumor
tunnel tunnel
turn (traffic) keren
turn down (volume, heat) lager
  zetten
turn off uitzetten
turn on aanzetten
turn up hoger zetten
tweezers pincet
twist (ankle) verstuiken
typical typisch

U

U.K. Groot-Brittannië
U.S. Verenigde Staten
ugly lelijk
ulcer zweer
umbrella paraplu
unconscious bewusteloos
under onder
underground station
  [BE] metrostation
understand begrijpen
unemployed werkeloos
units (phone card) eenheden
until tot

upstairs boven
urgent dringend
use n gebruik; v gebruiken
username gebruikersnaam

V

vacant vrij
vacation vakantie
vacuum cleaner stofzuiger
valet service parkeerdienst
valid geldig
validate (general) bevestigen;
  (ticket) afstempelen
valuable waardevol
value waarde
VAT [BE] BTW
vegan veganist
vegetarian n vegetariër; adj
  vegetarisch
vehicle voertuig
vein ader
version versie
very heel
video game videospelletje
view uitzicht
viewpoint uitkijkpunt
village dorp
vineyard wijngaard
visa visum
visit n bezoek; v bezoeken
visiting hours bezoekuur
visually impaired slechtziend
volleyball volleybal
voltage voltage
vomit n braaksel; v overgeven

W

wait wachten
waiting room wachtkamer
waiter kelner
waitress kelnerin
wake (self) wakker worden;
  (someone) wakker maken
wake-up service wekdienst
Wales Wales
walk (general) lopen;
  (on trail/path) wandelen
wall muur
wallet portemonnee
ward (hospital) afdeling
warm *adj* warm; *v* opwarmen
war memorial oorlogsmonument
warning waarschuwing
washable wasbaar
washing machine wasmachine
watch (timepiece) horloge
water water
water skis waterski's
waterfall waterval
waterproof waterdicht
wave golf
way weg
wear dragen
weather weer
weather forecast weerbericht
wedding huwelijk
week week
weekday weekdag
weekend weekend
weekend rate weekendtarief
weekly wekelijks

weigh wegen
weight gewicht
welcome welkom
west west
wetsuit duikerspak
what wat
wheelchair rolstoel
wheelchair ramp rolstoelopgang
when wanneer
where waar
which welke
while terwijl
who wie
whose van wie
why waarom
wide breed
wife vrouw
wildlife dieren in het wild
wind wind
windbreaker windjack
windmill molen
windscreen voorruit
windsurfing windsurfen
windy winderig
window (general) raam;
  (shop) etalage
window seat plaats bij het raam
wine wijn
wine list wijnkaart
wipe vegen
wireless draadloos
wish wens
with met
withdraw (money) opnemen
withdrawal (money) geldopname
within (time) binnen

without zonder
witness getuige
wood (forest) bos; **(material)** hout
wool wol
work (function) *n* werk
  v werken; **(operate)** bedienen
wrap *v* inpakken
write schrijven
wrong verkeerd

year jaar
yes ja
yesterday gisteren
yield (traffic) voorrang verlenen
you (sing. for.) u; **(sing. inf.)** jij;
  (pl. for.) u; **(pl. inf.)** jullie
young jong
youth jongeren
youth hostel jeugdherberg

X

x-ray röntgenfoto

Y

yacht jacht

Z

zebra crossing [BE] zebrapad
zero nul
zipper ritssluiting
zoo dierentuin

Dutch–English Dictionary

A

aanbevelen recommend
aandringen insist
aangetekend registered (mail)
aangeven declare
aankleden v dress
aankomst arrivals
aansteker n lighter
aantrekkelijk attractive
aanvaarden accept
aanval attack
aanvang start
aanwijzen indicate
aanwijzingen directions (map)
aanzetten turn on
aardewerk pottery
aardig pleasant
accepteren accept
accijns duty
accu battery
achter behind
achterkant back (opposite of front)
acupunctuur acupuncture
adapter adapter
ademhalen breathe
ader vein
adres address
advocaat lawyer
afdeling department (general);
  ward (hospital)
afdrukken print
afhalen to go (food) [take away BE]

afleveren deliver (bring)
aflopen v end
afmeting measurement
afrit exit ramp
afschuwelijk awful
afslag highway [motorway BE] exit
afsluiten v lock
afspraak appointment
afstand distance
afstempelen validate
aftershave aftershave
afval trash [rubbish BE]
afwasmachine dishwasher
airco air conditioning
akkoord gaan agree
al already
alle all
alleen only (merely); alone
  (without company)
allergie allergy
allergisch allergic
alstublieft (a.u.b.) please
alternatief alternative
altijd always
aluminiumfolie aluminum
  [kitchen BE] foil
ambachten handicrafts
ambassade embassy
ambassadeur ambassador
ambulance ambulance
Amerikaan n American
Amerikaans adj American
andere other
annuleren cancel
ansichtkaart post card
antacidum antacid
antibiotica antibiotics

antiek antique
antiseptisch *adj* antiseptic
antivries antifreeze
annuleren cancel
apart separate
apparatuur equipment
appartement apartment
apotheek pharmacy [chemist BE]
arm arm
armband bracelet
aromatherapie aromatherapy
arriveren arrive
artritis arthritis
asbak ashtray
aspirine aspirin
assistentie assistance
astma asthma
atletiek athletics
audiogids audio guide
Australië Australia
authentiek authentic
auto car
autodek car deck (ferry)
autosnelweg highway
  [motorway BE]
autoverhuur car rental [car hire BE]
avond evening
avondeten dinner
avondkleding formal wear

B

baan job
baby baby
babybox playpen
babydoekjes baby wipes
babyvoeding baby food

bad bath
badkamer bathroom
badmeester life guard (pool)
bagageafhaalruimte baggage claim
bagage luggage [baggage BE]
bagagedepot luggage
  [baggage BE] check
bagagekluisjes luggage lockers
bagagewagentje luggage cart
  [baggage trolley BE]
bakkerij bakery
bal ball
balkon balcony
ballet ballet
band band
bank bank
banketbakker pastry shop
bar bar
basketbal basketball
batterij battery
bed bed
beddengoed bedding
bedienen work (operate)
bediening service
bediening inbegrepen service
  included
bedieningsgeld service charge
bedrag amount
bedrijf company (business)
bedrijvencomplex business center
beekje stream
been leg
beet bite
beginnen *v* begin
beginner beginner
begraafplaats cemetery

begrijpen understand
beha bra
behalve except
behandeling treatment
belangrijk important
belastingvrij duty free
België Belgium
bellen call
benzine gas [petrol BE]
benzinestation gas [petrol BE] station
benzinetank gas tank
bereiken reach
berg mountain
bericht message
beroemd famous
beroep profession
beroven rob
beschikbaar available
beschrijven describe
besmettelijk contagious
bestellen v order
bestemming destination
bestuurder driver
betalen pay
betaling payment
betekenen v mean
betrouwbaar reliable
bevatten contain
bevestigen confirm
bevriezen freeze
bevroren frozen
bewaren keep
bewegen move
bewust conscious
bewusteloos unconscious

bezem broom
bezet taken
bezienswaardigheid sight (attraction)
bezitten v own
bezoek n visit
bezoeken v visit
bezoekuur visiting hours
bibliotheek library
bijgewerkt updated
bijknippen v trim
bijna almost
bijten bite
bijziend near-sighted [short-sighted BE]
bikini bikini
binnen inside
binnenbad Indoor pool
binnenkomen enter
binnenkomst entrance
binnenlands domestic
bioscoop movie theater [cinema BE]
bitter bitter
bizar bizarre
blaar blister
blaas bladder
bladeren browse
blauwe plek bruise
bleekmiddel bleach
blij happy
blijven stay
blikopener can opener
blind blind
blindedarm appendix
bloed blood
bloedarmoede anemia

bloeddruk blood pressure
bloedgroep blood group
bloeden bleed
bloem flower
bloemenwinkel flower shop
bloemist florist
bloes blouse
blokkeren v block
blootstellen expose
boarden boarding (airport)
boardingkaart boarding card
bocht curve
boek book
boekwinkel bookstore
boerderij farm
boete fine (police)
boksen boxing
bon receipt
boodschappen n shopping
boom tree
boottocht boat trip
bord plate
borgsom deposit
borst breast
borst geven breastfeed
borstel hairbrush
borstkas chest
bos forest
bot bone
botanische tuin botanical garden
bouwen build
boven above
bovenkant top
braaksel n vomit
brand n fire
brandalarm fire alarm
brandblusser fire extinguisher

branddeur fire door
brandstof fuel
brandtrap fire exit
brandweer fire department
[brigade BE]
brandweerkazerne fire station
brandwond burn
breed wide
breken v break
breuk fracture
brief letter
brievenbus mailbox [postbox BE]
bril glasses (optical)
Brit n British
Brits adj British
Britse pond pound sterling
broche brooch
brochure brochure
broer brother
brommer moped
brug bridge
bruin brown
bruinen v tan
buiten outside
buitenbad outdoor pool
buitenlands foreign
buitenlijn outside line (phone)
buiten werking out of order
buitenwijk suburb
bus bus
busbaan bus lane
bushalte bus stop
bushokje bus shelter
business class businessclass
busroute bus route
busstation bus station
butagas butane gas

C

cadeau gift
cadeauwinkel gift store
café cafe
calorie calorie
camper mobile home
camping campsite
Canada Canada
capsule capsule (medication)
casino casino
cd CD
cd-speler CD player
certificaat certificate
chauffeur driver
check-in balie check-in desk (airport)
chemisch toilet chemical toilet
circuit racetrack
claxon horn
club club
code code
collect call collect call [reversed charges BE]
collega colleague
commissie commission
compact compact
computer computer
concert concert
concertgebouw concert hall
concessie concession
concierge concierge
conditioner conditioner
condoom condom
conducteur ticket inspector
conferentie conference
conferentiezaal conference room

congres convention
congresgebouw convention hall
constant constant
constipatie constipation
consulaat consulate
contactlens contact lens
contactlensvloeistof contact lens solution
contant cash
controle n control
cosmetisch cosmetic
coupé compartment (train)
couvert cover charge
creditcard credit card
cruise n cruise
cruisen v cruise

D

daar there
dag day (time period); hello; goodbye
dagelijks daily
dak roof
dames women's restroom
dameskapper hairdresser
dameskleding ladieswear
dan then (time)
danken thank
dans n dance
dansen v dance
dat that
decoratief decorative
defect faulty
deken blanket
delen v share
Delfts blauw Delft blue

delicatessen delicatessen
denken think
deodorant deodorant
deposito deposit
detail detail
deur door
De heer (Dhr.) Mr.
de weg wijzen *v* direct
diamant diamond
diarree diarrhea
dichtbij near
dieet diet
dief thief
diefstal theft
dienblad tray
dienst *n* service
diep deep
diepvriezer freezer
dier animal
dierentuin zoo
diesel diesel
digitaal digital
dij thigh
dik thick
dineren dine
ding thing
directeur director
dirigent conductor
discotheek dance club
discountzaak discount store
dobbelsteen dice
doel purpose
dok dock
dokter doctor
donker dark
doodlopende weg dead end
doof deaf

dood dead
door through (movement);
  by (by means of)
doorgaand verkeer through traffic
doorlopend continuous
doorslikken swallow
doorspoelen *v* flush
doos box
dorp village
dorstig thirsty
dosering dosage
douane customs
douaneaangifteformulier
  customs declaration form
douanecontrole customs control
douche shower
dozijn dozen
draadloos wireless
draaien *v* turn (general); play
  (movie)
dragen wear (clothes)
drankje *n* drink
dringend urgent
drinken *v* drink
drogist drugstore [chemist BE]
dronken drunk
droog dry
druk busy
drukken press (clothing)
druppel drop (medication)
druppelen drip
duikbril goggles
duiken *v* dive
duikerspak wetsuit
duim thumb
duizelig dizzy
dun thin

duren *v* take (time)
duur expensive
duwen push
dweil mop

E

echt real
echtgenoot spouse (male)
echtgenote spouse (female)
echtheid authenticity
eenheden units (phone card)
eenpersoonskamer single room
eenrichtingsstraat one-way street
eenrichtingsverkeer one-way (traffic)
eerst first
eerste klas first class
eerstehulp (EHBO) first aid
eetkamer dining room
eetlust appetite
eigen *adj* own
eigendom property
einde *n* end
elektrisch electric
elektronisch electronic
elk every
e-mail e-mail
e-mailadres e-mail address
en and
Engeland England
Engels English
enkeltje one-way [single BE] ticket
envelop envelope
epileptisch epileptic
ergens somewhere
ernstig serious

ervaring experience
essentieel essential
eten eat
e-ticket e-ticket
euro euro
Eurocheque Eurocheque
even briefly
evenement event
exact exact
excursie tour
expres express
extra *adj* additional

F

faciliteiten facilities
factor factor
familie family
fastfood fast food
favoriet favorite
fax fax
faxapparaat fax machine
faxnummer fax number
feestdag holiday
feestje party (social)
fiets bicycle
fietspad bicycle path
fietsen cycling
fietsroute bicycle route
fijn nice
file traffic jam
film film (camera); movie [film BE]
filter filter
fitnessruimte gym
flat apartment [flat BE]
flauwvallen *v* faint
fles bottle

flesopener bottle opener
flesvoeding formula (baby)
flits flash
floss dental floss
föhn hair dryer
fontein fountain
fooi tip
fopspeen pacifier [soother BE]
formulier form
fornuis stove
foto photograph
fotografie photography
fotorolletje film
fototoestel camera
fout mistake

G

gaan go
gaas gauze
galerie gallery
gang hallway (building); course (meal)
gangpad aisle
garage garage
garantie guarantee
garderobe coat check
gat hole
gate gate (airport)
gauw soon
gay club gay club
gebeuren happen
geboortedatum date of birth
geboren born
gebouw building
gebroken broken
gebruik *n* use

gebruiken *v* use
gebruikersnaam username
gebruiksaanwijzing instructions
gedenkteken memorial
geduldig *adj* patient
geel yellow
geen no
gefeliciteerd congratulations
gehandicapt disabled
geheugenkaart memory card
gehoorapparaat hearing aid
gekoeld refrigerated
geld money
geldig valid
geldautomaat ATM
geldopname withdrawal (money)
geldwisselkantoor currency exchange
geleden ago
geleidehond guide dog
gelijk *adv* level
gelukkig fortunately
genoeg enough
geopend open
gepensioneerd retired
geschenk gift
geschikt voor de magnetron microwaveable
geschikt suitable
getuige witness
geur smell
gevaarlijk dangerous
gevecht *n* fight
geven give
gevonden voorwerpen lost and found [lost property office BE]
gevorderd advanced

gewicht weight

gewricht *n* joint

gezelschap company (companionship)

gezicht face

gezichtsbehandeling *n* facial

gezin family (immediate)

gezondheid health

gezwel lump

gids guide (tour, book)

gif poison

gift donation

gisteren yesterday

gitaar guitar

glad icy

glas glass (drinking)

gloeilamp light bulb

gluten gluten

godsdienst religion

goed *adj* good

goederen freight

goedkeuren approve

goedkoop cheap

golf golf (game); wave (water)

golfbaan golf course

golfstok golf club

gootsteen sink

gordijn curtain

goud gold

graad degree

gracht canal

gram gram

grap joke

grappig funny

gras grass

grasduinen browse

gratis free of charge

graveren engrave

griep flu

groentewinkel produce store [greengrocer BE]

groep group

grondzeil groundcloth [groundsheet BE]

groot large

Groot-Brittannië Great Britain

grot cave

gymschoenen sneakers

gynaecoloog gynecologist

H

haar hair

haarspray hairspray

haast *n* rush

haasten *v* rush

hal hall (general); lobby (theater, hotel)

halal halal

hallo hello

half half

halsketting necklace

halte stop (bus, tram)

hamer hammer

hand hand

handbagage carry-on [hand BE] luggage

handdoek towel

handschoenen gloves

handtas purse [handbag BE]

handwerkwinkel craft shop

hangslot padlock

hard hard

hart heart

hartaanval heart attack

hartkloppingen palpitations
hartkwaal heart condition
haven harbor
hebben have
heel very
heerlijk lovely
heet hot
hek gate
helft *n* half
helling incline
helm helmet
helpen help
herenkapper barber
herenkleding menswear
herentoilet men's restroom
herhalen repeat
herinneren remember
hersenschudding concussion
hetzelfde same
heuvel hill
hier here
hij he
historisch historical
hobby hobby
hoe how
hoed hat
hoek corner
hoest *n* cough
hoesten *v* cough
hoeveel how much; how many
hoeveelheid amount
hoger zetten turn up
hond dog
honger hunger
hongerig hungry
honkbal baseball

hoofd head
hoofdpijn headache
hoofdweg main road
hoogte height
hooikoorts hay fever
horen hear
horloge watch
hotel hotel
houden keep
houden van *v* love
hout wood
houten hamer mallet
houtskool charcoal
huid skin
huis house
huishoudfolie plastic wrap
[cling film BE]
hulp assistance
hulpdienst emergency service
huren rent
hut cabin
huurauto rental car
huwelijk wedding
huwelijksreis honeymoon

I

iemand someone
Ierland Ireland
iets something
ijsbaan skating rink
ijssalon ice-cream parlor
ijshockey ice hockey
ijzerwarenwinkel hardware store
ik I
illegaal illegal
imitatie imitation

in in
inbegrepen included (price)
ibuprofen ibuprofen
incheckbalie check-in desk
inchecken check-in
indigestie indigestion
infectie infection
informeel informal
informeren notify
informatie information
informatiebalie information desk
informatiebureau information office
ingang entrance
inhalen v pass
inhaalverbod no-passing zone
injectie injection
inloggen log on
innemen take (medication)
inpakken pack (suitcase); wrap (present)
inreisvisum entry visa
inrijden enter (traffic)
insectenbeet insect bite
insectenspray insect repellent
inslaan break
instant messenger instant messenger
instappers loafers
instorten collapse
instructeur instructor
insuline insulin
intensive care intensive care
interessant interesting
interesse interest (hobby)
internationaal international

Internationale Studentenkaart International Student Card
internet internet
internetcafé internet cafe
internetverbinding internet service
intoetsen enter
invullen fill out
invoegen merge (traffic)
invoeren insert
inwendig internally
inwerpen insert
inwoner resident
inwoners van de EU EU citizens

J

ja yes
jaar year
jaar oud aged
jacht yacht
jagen hunt
jas coat
jasje jacket
jazz jazz
jetlag jet lag
jetski jet-ski
jeugdherberg youth hostel
jeuk n itch
jij you (informal)
jodium iodine
jong young
jongen boy
jongeren youth
juist correct
jurk n dress
juwelier jeweler

kaak jaw
kaars candle
kaart card (credit card); map (directions)
kaartje ticket
kakkerlak cockroach
kalender calendar
kalmerend middel sedative
kam comb
kamer room
kamermeisje maid (hotel)
kamertarief room rate
kamperen v camp
kampvuur fire
kan jug
kanaal canal
kanker cancer
kanovaren canoeing
kant lace
kantoor office
kantoorbenodigdheden office supplies
kapot broken
kapper barber; hairdresser
kapsel hair cut
karaf carafe
kassa checkout; cash register
kassajuffrouw cashier
kasteel castle
kater hangover
kathedraal cathedral
keel throat
katoen cotton
keelpijn sore throat
keer time

kelder basement
kelner waiter
kelnerin waitress
kenmerk feature
kennen know
keramiek ceramics
kerk church
kerkdienst n service
ketel kettle
ketting chain
keuken kitchen
keukenpapier paper towel
kies v dial (phone)
kiespijn toothache
kijken v look
kilo kilo
kilometer kilometer
kind child
kinderarts pediatrician
kinderkleding children's clothing
kindermenu children's menu
kinderportie children's portion
kinderstoel highchair
kinderwagen stroller [pushchair BE]
kinderzitje car seat
kinderzwembad kiddie [paddling BE] pool
kiosk newsstand [news agent BE]
klaar ready
klanteninformatie customer information
klantenservice customer service
klas class
klederdracht costume (local)
kledingwinkel clothing store
klerenhanger coat hanger
klein small

klem clamp
kleur color
klier gland
klif cliff
kliniek clinic
klok clock
klomp *n* clog
klooster monastery
kloppen knock
kluis safe
knie knee
knippen *v* cut
knoop button
koekenpan frying pan
koel cool (temperature)
koelkast refrigerator
koerier courier
koffer suitcase
kok *n* cook
kom bowl
komen come
kookgelegenheid cooking facilities
koopje bargain
koorts fever
kopen buy
koper copper
kopie *n* photocopy
kopieerapparaat photocopier
kopiëren *v* photocopy
kopje cup
kort short
korte broek shorts
korting discount
koosjer kosher
kosten *v* cost
koud *adj* cold
kousen stockings

kraan faucet [tap BE]
kraanwater tap water
kramp cramps
krant newspaper
krap tight
krijgen get (receive)
kristal crystal
kroon crown (dental)
kruidenierswinkel grocery store [greengrocer BE]
kruier porter
kruis *n* cross
kruispunt intersection [junction BE]
krukken crutches
kwitantie receipt
kuil pothole (road)
kunnen *v* can
kunstenaar artist
kunstgalerie art gallery
kunstgebit denture
kurkentrekker corkscrew
kussen *n* pillow; *v* kiss
kust coast
kuuroord spa
kwaliteit quality
kwart quarter
kwijt missing

L

laag low
laantje lane
laarzen boots
laat late
laatste last
label label
lactose-intolerant lactose intolerant
ladder ladder

lager zetten turn down (volume, heat)
laken sheet
lamp lamp
land country
landen *v* land
landnummer country code
lang long
lange broek pants [trousers BE]
langzaam slow
laten zien show
lawaaierig noisy
laxerend middel laxative
ledikant cot
leeg *adj* empty (general); dead (battery)
leegmaken *v* empty
leer leather
legaal legal
legitimatiebewijs ID
lekken *v* leak
lekker delicious
lelijk ugly
lenen borrow (from); lend (to)
lengte height (person); length (general)
lens lens
lensdop lens cap
lepel spoon
leren learn
les lesson
leuk vinden enjoy
leunen lean
leven life
lever liver
levering delivery
lezen read

licht light
lichten headlights (car)
lichting collection (mail)
lid member
liefde *n* love
lift elevator [lift BE]
ligstoel deck chair
lijn line
limousine limousine
links left
linnen linen
lip lip
lippenstift lipstick
liter liter
logeren stay (overnight)
logies accommodations
logies-ontbijt bed and breakfast
lokaal local
loket ticket office
long lung
longontsteking pneumonia
loodvrij unleaded (gasoline)
lopen *v* walk
los loose
losschroeven unscrew
loterij lottery
lucht air
luchtbed air mattress
luchtpomp air pump
luchtpost airmail
luchtvaartmaatschappij airline
luchtziekte airsickness
lucifers matches
luid loud
luier diaper [nappy BE]
luik shutter
lunch lunch

maag stomach
maagpijn stomachache
maaltijd meal
maand month
maandverband sanitary napkin [pad BE]
maar but
maat size
maatbeker measuring cup
maatlepel measuring spoon
machine machine
magnetron microwave (oven)
magnifiek magnificent
maken make
make-up make-up
makkelijk easy
man man; husband
manager manager
mand basket
manicure manicure
mannelijk male
markt market
mascara mascara
masker mask
massage massage
matinee matinee
matras mattress
mededelingenbord bulletin board
medicijn medication
medische nooddienst emergency medical service
meedoen join
meegaan accompany (go with); last (keep)
meenemen *v* take

meer *n* lake; *adj* more
meisje girl
meneer Mr.
menstruatie period
menstruatiepijn menstrual cramps
menukaart menu
mes knife
met with
metaal metal
meten measure
metro subway [underground BE]
metrostation subway [underground BE] station
meubels furniture
Mevrouw Mrs.; madam
middag afternoon
middernacht midnight
migraine migraine
mijn mine
minder less
minibar mini-bar
minimum minimum
minuut minute
mis mass
misschien maybe
misselijk nauseous
misselijkheid nausea
mist fog
misverstand misunderstanding
mobiel cell [mobile BE] phone
modern contemporary
moe tired
moeilijk difficult
moeras swamp
moeten must
mogelijk possible
mogen *v* can

mok mug
molen windmill
mond mouth
monteur mechanic
mooi beautiful
morgen tomorrow
moskee mosque
motor engine
motorboot motorboat
motorfiets motorcycle
mountainbike mountain bike
mouw sleeve
muggenbeet mosquito bite
munt coin
museum museum
muur wall
muziek music

N

na after
naaien sew
naam *n* name
naar to
naast next to
nacht night
nachtapotheek all-night pharmacy
nachtclub night club
nagel nail
nagelsalon nail salon
nagelvijl nail file
nagesynchroniseerd dubbed
nat wet
nationaliteit nationality
natuur nature
natuurpad nature trail
natuurreservaat nature reserve
Nederlands Dutch (language)

Nederlanders Dutch (people)
nee no
neerzetten put
nek neck
nemen *v* take
netnummer area code
netwerk network
neus nose
niemand nobody
nier kidney
niet do not; not
niet-EU-ingezetenen non-EU-citizens
niet-roken non-smoking
niets nothing
nieuw new
nieuws news
Nieuw-Zeeland New Zealand
nodig necessary
nodig hebben need
nog *adv* still
non-stop non-stop
noodgeval emergency
noodrem emergency brake
nooduitgang emergency exit
nooit never
noord north
normaal normal; regular (gas)
nu now
nul zero
nummer number
nylon nylon

O

ochtend morning
of or
ogenblik moment

oké OK

olie oil

om at (time)

omdat because

omhelzen hug

omleiding detour [diversion BE]

onbeleefd rude

onbeperkt unlimited

onbevoegd unauthorized

onder under

ondertiteld subtitled

onderzoek examination

ondiep shallow

ongelijk uneven (ground)

ongelooflijk incredible

ongeluk accident

ongeveer about (approximately)

onschuldig innocent

ontbijt breakfast

ontdooien defrost

onthouden remember

ontmoeten meet

ontmoetingsplaats meeting place [point BE]

ontruimen vacate (room)

ontsteken infect

ontsteking inflammation

ontstopper plunger

onttrekken v extract

ontvangen receive

ontvangstcentrum reception center

ontwikkelen develop

ontwrichten dislocate

onvergezeld unaccompanied

onze our

onzin nonsense

oog eye

ook also

oom uncle

oor ear

oorbellen earrings

oordruppels ear drops

oorlogsmonument war memorial

oorpijn earache

oost east

op on

opdienen serve

open adj open

openbaar public

opendoen v open (window)

openen v open

openingstijden office hours

openlucht adj outdoor

openmaken open

opera opera

operatie operation

opgezet swollen

ophalen v pick up

oplossen dissolve

opnemen withdraw (money)

oppas babysitter

oppassen caution; beware

oprit entrance ramp (highway)

oproep call

opruiming clearance; sale

opslaan save (computer)

opstaan stand up

opstijgen take off (plane)

opvullen fill up

opticien optician

opwarmen v warm

organiseren organize

origineel original

orkest orchestra
oud old
oudere senior citizens
ouders parents
ovaal oval
oven oven
over about
overbagage excess luggage [baggage BE]
overdekt indoor
overgeven v vomit
overhemd shirt (men's)
overstappen v change (bus)
oversteken v cross
overtocht crossing

P

paar pair
paard horse
paardenrenbaan horsetrack
paardrijden horseback riding
paars purple
pad path
pak suit
pakket package [parcel BE]
paleis palace
panorama panorama
pantoffels slippers
paracetamol acetaminophen [paracetamol BE]
parasol umbrella (sun) [sunshade BE]
paraplu umbrella (rain)
parel pearl
park park
parkeer en reis park and ride
parkeerdienst valet service

parkeergarage parking garage [car park BE]
parkeermeter parking meter
parkeerplaats parking lot [car park BE]
parkeerplek parking space
parkeerbon parking ticket
parkeerverbod no parking
parkeren parking
particulier private
parttime part time
paskamer fitting room
paspoort passport
passagier passenger
passen try on (clothes)
patiënt n patient
pauze intermission
paviljoen pavilion
pech breakdown (car)
pedicure pedicure
pen pen
penicilline penicillin
pensioen retirement [pension BE]
pension guesthouse
per per
per expres express mail
periode period
persen v press
personeel staff
persoon person
picknick picnic
pijn n pain
pijn hebben v hurt
pijnlijk sore
pijp pipe
pil pill
PIN PIN

pincet tweezers
pizzeria pizzeria
plaats place (location); seat (on train, etc.)
plaatselijk local
plak slice
plan plan
plant *n* plant
planten *v* plant
plastic plastic
plat flat
platina platinum
plein square
pleister bandage [plaster BE]
plezier fun
plug plug
polikliniek health clinic
politie police
politiebureau police station
polyester polyester
pomp pump
pond pound
populair popular
porselein porcelain
portemonnee wallet
portie portion
post *n* mail
posten *v* mail
postkantoor post office
posttarief postage
postwissel money order
postzegel *n* stamp
pot pot
praktijk practice
praten talk
prepaidkaart prepaid phone card
pretpark amusement park

prijs price
prijsverlaging discount
prima fine (good)
primus kerosene stove
privé private
probleem problem
proces-verbaal police report
proeven *v* taste
programma program
proost cheers
pub pub
publiek public
pyjama pajamas

R

raam window
raadplegen consult
racket racket (tennis)
rapport report
reactie reaction
recept prescription
receptie reception
receptionist receptionist
recht straight
rechts right (direction)
rechtstreeks *adj* direct
reddingsboot life boat
reddingsgordel life preserver [belt BE]
reddingsvest life jacket
reduceren reduce
reformproducten health food
reformwinkel health food store
regen *n* rain
regenen *v* rain
regenjas raincoat
relatie relationship

reis trip
reisbureau travel agency
reischeque traveler's check
[cheque BE]
reisgids tour guide
reisorganisator tour operator
reisziekte motion sickness
[travel sickness BE]
reizen travel
rekening bill
rem brake
renbaan racetrack [race course BE]
rennen run
renovatie renovation
reparatie *n* repair
repareren *v* repair
reserveren *v* reserve
reservering reservation
reserveringsbalie reservation desk
reservoir reservoir
restaurant restaurant
restauratiewagen dining car (train)
retourtje round-trip [return BE]
ticket
richting direction
riem belt
rietje straw
rij line [queue BE]
rijbaan lane
rijbewijs driver's license
rijden drive
rijstrook lane
ring ring
ritssluiting zipper
rivier river
roeiboot rowboat

roeien row
roestvrij staal stainless steel
route route
rok skirt
roken *v* smoke; smoking
section (restaurant)
rokerszone smoking area
rolstoel wheelchair
rolstoelopgang wheelchair ramp
roltrap escalator
roman novel
romantisch romantic
rond round (shape); around
(direction)
rondleiding guided tour
rondvaart boat trip
röntgenfoto x-ray
roomservice room service
roos rose
rotonde traffic circle
[roundabout BE]
rots rock
route route
roze pink
rug back (body part)
rugby rugby
rugpijn backache
rugzak backpack
ruilen exchange
ruimte space
rusten *v* rest
ruïne ruins
rustgebied rest area
rustig quiet

's avonds in the evening
's middags p.m.
's morgens a.m.
sms'en *v* text messaging
saai boring
sandalen sandals
satijn satin
sauna sauna
schaakspel chess
schaal scale
schaar scissors
schaatsen *n* skates; *v* ice-skating
schade damage
schadeclaim insurance claim
schaduw shade
schattig cute
scheerapparaat razor
scheerkwast shaving brush
scheermesje razor blade
scheerzeep shaving cream
scheiden divorce
schep shovel
scheren shave
scherp sharp
scheuren tear (muscle)
schilderij painting
schip ship
schoen shoe
schoenenwinkel shoe store
schoenmaker shoe repair
schok shock
schoon clean
schoonmaakmiddelen cleaning supplies
Schotland Scotland

schouder shoulder
schrijven write
schroevendraaier screwdriver
seks sex
selecteren choose
seminar seminar
servet napkin
shampoo shampoo
sieraden jewelry
siertegel decorative tile
sigaar cigar
sigarenwinkel tobacconist
sigaret cigarette
single single (person)
sjaal scarf
slaapkamer bedroom
slaappil sleeping pill
slaapwagen sleeping car [sleeper car BE]
slaapzak sleeping bag
slabbetje bib
slager butcher
slagveld battle site
slapeloosheid insomnia
slapen sleep
slecht bad
slechts only
slechthorend hearing impaired
slechtziend visually impaired
sleutel key
sleutelkaart key card
sleutelring key ring
slijter liquor store [off-licence BE]
slot *n* lock
sluiten *v* close
smaak *n* taste
smal narrow

smaragd emerald

snackbar snack bar

snel fast

snelheid speed

snelheidslimiet speed limit

snelweg highway [motorway BE]

sneeuw *n* snow

sneeuwen *v* snow

snijwond *n* cut

snoepwinkel candy store [confectioner BE]

snorkelen snorkle

sokken socks

soms sometimes

soort kind (type)

sorry sorry

soulmuziek soul music

souvenir souvenir

souvenirgids souvenir guide

souvenirwinkel souvenir store

spaarrekening savings account

spatel spatula

speciaal special

specialist specialist

speelgoed toy

speelgoedwinkel toy store

speelhal arcade

speeltuin playground

spelen play

spellen *v* spell

spelletje game

spiegel mirror

spier muscle

spijkerbroek jeans

spijkerstof denim

spitsuur rush hour

spons sponge

spoor platform

sport sport

sportwinkel sporting goods store

sportvereniging sports club

spreken speak

spreekkamer doctor's office [surgery BE]

spullen things

staal steel

staan stand

staanplaats standing room

stad town

stadhuis town hall

stadion stadium

stadscentrum downtown area

stadsplattegrond town map

stadsplein town square

standaard standard

standby-ticket stand-by ticket

starten *v* start

stadion stadium

standbeeld statue

station train [railway BE] station

steegje alley

steek bite (insect)

steelpan saucepan

steil steep

stelen steal

stempelen stamp

steriele oplossing sterilizing solution

sterk strong

sterling zilver sterling silver

steward flight attendant

stijf stiff

stijl *n* style

stilist stylist

stoep sidewalk [pavement BE]
stof fabric
stofzuiger vacuum cleaner
stomerij dry cleaner
stomen v steam
stopcontact electrical outlet
stoppen stop
stoplicht traffic light
storen disturb
straat street
strand beach
strandboulevard seafront
strandmeester lifeguard (beach)
streek region
strijken v iron
strijkijzer n iron
strippenkaart bus ticket
stroom stream (flow); electricity (power)
stroomversnelling rapids
stropdas n tie
student student
studeren study
stuifmeelgehalte pollen count
stuk piece
stylen v style
sufheid drowsiness
suikerpatiënt diabetic
sun-block sun-block cream
super premium (gas) [super BE]
supermarkt supermarket
surfplank surfboard
sweatshirt sweatshirt
symbool symbol
symptoom symptom
synagoge synagogue
synthetisch synthetic

T

T-shirt T-shirt
tv TV
taai tough
taalcursus language course
taalgids phrase book
tabak tobacco
tablet tablet
tafel table
takelwagen tow truck
tampon tampon
tand tooth
tandarts dentist
tandartspraktijk dental office
tandenborstel toothbrush
tandpasta toothpaste
tapijt carpet
tas bag
taxi taxi
taxistandplaats taxi stand [rank BE]
te too
team team
techniek engineering
teen toe
tegel tile
tegenover opposite
te kauwen chewable
tekenen v sign (signature)
te koop for sale
tekst n text
telefoneren v call (phone)
telefonist telephone operator
telefoon telephone
telefoongesprek phone call
telefoongids phone directory
telefoonkaart phone card

telefoonnummer phone number
telefoonzuil pay phone
temperatuur temperature
tenger petite
tenminste at least
tennis tennis
tennisbaan tennis court
tent tent
tentharing tent peg
tentstok tent pole
terminal terminal
terugbetaling refund *n*
terugbrengen *v* return (thing)
terugkomen *v* return (person)
terwijl while
theater theater
theelepel teaspoon
thermometer thermometer
thermosfles thermos
thuis home
tijd time
tijdschrift magazine
tin pewter
tint tint
tissue tissue
toebehoren belong
toegang access; admission
toegangsprijs admission charge
toestaan *v* permit
tourist tourist
toeristische rondrit sightseeing tour
toernooi tournament
toeslag surcharge
toestel extension (phone)
toezicht supervision
toilet restroom [toilet BE]

toiletpapier toilet paper
tol toll
tolhuisje toll booth
tolk interpreter
tolweg toll road
toneelstuk play (theater)
tonen *v* show
tong tongue
toren tower
tot until
touringcar long-distance bus
touw rope
traditioneel traditional
tram tram
trap stairs
trein train
trekken pull
trottoir sidewalk [pavement BE]
trouwen marry
trui sweater
tuin garden
tumor tumor
tunnel tunnel
tussen between
twaalf uur 's middags noon
  [midday BE]
tweedehandswinkel
  secondhand store
tweede klas economy class
tweepersoonskamer double room

U

u you (formal)
uit from (destination); out (general)
uitchecken check out
uitgaan go out

218

uitgids entertainment guide
uitgang *n* exit
uitgeput exhausted
uitgeven spend
uitgezonderd except
uitkijkpunt vantage point, overlook
uitkleden undress
uitloggen log off
uitnodigen *v* invite
uitrit exit
uitrusting equipment
uitslag rash
uitsluitend exclusively
uitspreken pronounce
uitstappen get off
uitstekend terrific
uitverkocht sold out
uitzetten turn off
uitzicht view
uur hour

V

vaak *adv* frequent
vacature vacancy
vakantie vacation [holiday BE]
vakantiehuisje cottage
valhelm helmet
vallei valley
vallen *v* fall
valuta currency
vanavond tonight
vandaag today
vasthouden *v* hold
vast menu fixed-price menu
vechten *v* fight
veerboot ferry
veganist vegan

vegen wipe, sweep (clean)
vegetariër *n* vegetarian
vegetarisch *adj* vegetarian
veilig safe
veiligheid safety
veiligheidsgordel seat belt
veiligheidsspeld safety pin
veilig voor kinderen childproof
veld field
ventilator *n* fan
ver far
verband bandage
verbazingwekkend amazing
verbeteren improve
verbinding connection
verbinding maken connect
verbinding verbreken disconnect
verboden prohibited
verboden toegang keep out
verbreken disconnect
verdieping floor (level in building)
verdovingsmiddel anesthetic
verdrinken drown
verdwaald lost
vereist required
Verenigde Staten U.S.
verf paint
vergadering meeting
vergaderruimte meeting room
vergeten forget
vergoeden *v* refund
vergoeding *n* refund
vergunning permit
vergroten enlarge
verhuizen move
verhuren rent out

verjaardag birthday
verkeerd wrong
verkeer traffic
verkeersovertreding traffic violation [offence BE]
verkeersvrij gebied pedestrian zone [precinct BE]
verklaring statement
verkoop sale
verkopen sell
verkoudheid cold (flu)
verkrachting rape
verlamming paralysis
verliezen lose
verloofd engaged (marriage)
verloofde fiance
verloren lost
vermaken alter
verminderen reduce
verontschuldigen apologize
verpleegster nurse
verplicht mandatory
verrekken strain (muscle)
verrekijker binoculars
vers fresh
verschonen change (baby)
verschuldigd zijn owe
versie version
versnapering refreshment
versnelling gear
versperd blocked
verstellen mend (clothes)
verstopt blocked
verstuiken twist (ankle)
versturen send (general); mail (mail)
vertalen translate
vertaler translator

vertaling translation
vertellen tell
vertraagd delayed
vertraging delay
vertrek departures (airport)
vertrekgate departure gate
vertrekken v leave
vervaldatum expiration [expiry BE] date
vervangen replace
vervangingsonderdeel replacement part
vervelend unpleasant
verven v paint
vervoer transport
verwarming heat [heating BE]
verwijderen remove (general); delete (computer)
verwonden injure
verzekering insurance
verzekeringsbewijs insurance card [certificate BE]
verziend far-sighted [long-sighted BE]
videospelletje video game
vierkant square
vies dirty
vijver pond
vinden find
vinger finger
vissen fishing
visitekaartje business card
visum visa
vitrine display case
vlek stain
vlieg n fly
vliegen v fly

vliegtuig airplane
vliegveld airport
vlo flea
vlooienmarkt flea market
vlucht flight
vluchtinformatie flight information
vluchtnummer flight number
vochtig damp
vochtinbrengende crème moisturizer
voeden feed
voedsel food
voedselvergiftiging food poisoning
voelen feel
voertuig vehicle
voet foot
voetbal soccer [football BE]
voetganger pedestrian
voetgangersgebied traffic-free zone
voetgangersoversteekplaats pedestrian crossing
voetpad footpath
vogel bird
vol full
volgen follow
volgende next
volleybal volleyball
voltage voltage
volwassene adult
voor before (time)
voorbeeld example
voorbehoedsmiddel contraceptive
voordat before
voorkant front
voorrang right of way
voorrang verlenen yield [give way BE]

voorruit windshield [windscreen BE]
voorstellen introduce (person); suggest (subject)
voorstelling performance
voortreffelijk superb
voorzichtig careful
vorige *adj* last
vork fork
vorm shape
vrachtwagen truck [lorry BE]
vragen ask
vreemd strange
vreselijk terrible
vriend friend (male); boyfriend
vriendelijk friendly
vriendin friend (female); girlfriend
vrij free (no charge); vacant (unoccupied)
vroeg early
vrouw woman; wife
vrouwelijk female
vuilnis trash [rubbish BE]
vuilniszak trash bag
vullen fill
vulling filling
vuur fire
vuurtoren lighthouse
VVV tourist office

W

waar where (location); true (accurate)
waarde value
waardevol valuable
waarschuwing warning
wachten wait
wachtkamer waiting room

wachtwoord password
wagentje cart [trolley BE]
wagon car
wakker maken wake (someone)
Wales Wales
wandelen walking (general); hiking (on trail)
wandelpad walkway; trail (nature)
wandelroute walking route
wandeluitrusting hiking gear
wanneer when
warenhuis department store
warme bron hot spring
wasbaar washable
wasknijper peg
wasmachine washing machine
wasmiddel detergent
wassen wash
wasserette laundromat [launderette BE]
wasserij laundry service
wastafel sink
wat what
water water
waterski's water skis
waterskiën waterskiing
waterdicht waterproof
waterval waterfall
wedden bet
wedstrijd contest (general); game (sport)
weduwe widowed (female)
weduwnaar widowed (male)
week week
weekdag weekday
weekend weekend
weekendtarief weekend rate

weer weather
weerbericht weather forecast
weg *n* road; *adv* away
wegen weigh
wegenkaart road map
wegwerpbaar disposable
weiland field
weinig few
wekdienst wake-up call service
wekker alarm clock
welke which
welkom welcome
wenkbrauw eyebrow
wens wish
werk *n* work
werkeloos unemployed
werken *v* work
wesp wasp
west west
wie who
wieg crib [child's cot BE]
wielerwedstrijd cycling race
wielklem clamp
wij we
wijngaard vineyard
wijnkaart wine list
wijnproeven wine tasting
wijzigen *v* change
wind wind
winderig windy
windjack windbreaker
windmolen windmill
windsurfen windsurfing
winkel store
winkelbediende shop assistant
winkelcentrum shopping mall [centre BE]

winkelen *v* shopping
winkelmandje shopping basket
winkelplattegrond store guide
[directory BE]
winkelwagentje shopping cart
[trolley BE]
wisselen exchange
wisselgeld change
wisselkantoor currency exchange
office
wisselkoers exchange rate
wit white
wol wool
wonen live
woonerf residential zone
woordenboek dictionary
worden become

Z

zakdoek handkerchief
zaken business
zakencentrum business district
zaklantaarn flashlight [torch BE]
zand sand
zebrapad crosswalk
[zebra crossing BE]
zee sea
zeep soap
zeespiegel sea level
zeeziek seasick
zeggen say
zekeringkast fuse box
zeldzaam rare
zeker sure
zelfbediening self-service
zelfgemaakt homemade

zelfstandig self-employed
zetpil suppository
ziek sick [ill BE]
ziekenhuis hospital
ziektekostenverzekeing health
insurance
zien see
zijde silk
zilver silver
zinsnede phrase
zitplaats seat
zitten sit
zoet sweet
zon sun
zonder without
zonnebaden sunbathe
zonnebrand sunburn
zonnebrandcrème sunscreen
zonnebril sunglasses
zonnesteek sunstroke
zout *n* salt; *adj* salty
zuid south
zuigfles baby bottle
zuivel dairy
zuivelproducten dairy products
zuiver pure
zuurstof oxygen
zwaar heavy
zwanger pregnant
zwelling swelling
zwembad swimming pool
zwembroek swimming trunks
zwemmen swimming
zwempak swimsuit
zwemvest life jacket